2 to 22 DAYS IN THE AMERICAN SOUTHWEST

THE ITINERARY PLANNER
1993 EDITION

RICHARD HARRIS

John Muir Publications
Santa Fe, New Mexico

Other JMP books by Richard Harris
2 to 22 Days in Florida
2 to 22 Days in the Pacific Northwest
2 to 22 Days in Texas

This book is for Rita Guidi-Morosini, artist, environmental activist, and steady source of insight and inspiration.

Special thanks to those who make it possible, including the Rio Grande chapter of the Sierra Club, Pamela Lanier and Julio Valdez, Anne Wright, Richard Polese, Daniel O'Keefe, and the National Park Service.

John Muir Publications, P.O. Box 613, Santa Fe, NM 87504

ISSN 1058-6075
ISBN 1-56261-080-5

Distributed to the book trade by:
W. W. Norton & Company, Inc.
New York, New York

Design Mary Shapiro
Maps Holly Wood
Cover Photo Leo de Wys Inc./Henryk Kaiser
Typography Copygraphics, Inc., Santa Fe, N.M.
Printer McNaughton & Gunn, Inc.

CONTENTS

The Southwest in 22 Days

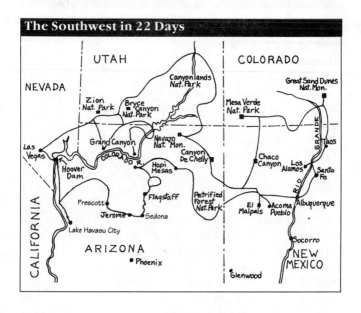

Under the ancient volcano in northern New Mexico lives the nation's largest community of nuclear physicists. Twelve miles to the east, the people of San Ildefonso Pueblo speak their Native American language, dance in time-honored ceremonies, and make pottery by methods a thousand years old. Five miles to the south, in the Bandelier wilderness, you can walk for three days without coming to a road.

Welcome to the American Southwest, where pristine wilderness and civilizations many centuries old endure side by side with "Star Wars" technology. *2 to 22 Days in the American Southwest* contains a self-guided travel itinerary for a three-week road trip that will take you to the most fascinating places in New Mexico, Arizona, and the southern parts of Colorado, Utah, and Nevada. The tour follows a 3,000-mile meandering loop, mostly on less-used secondary highways. It intersects Interstate 40 several times and connects with Interstates 15, 25, and 70, so it's easy to join and leave from any direction.

If you have less than three weeks to explore, use any of the route's various segments as a relaxing scenic alternative to I-40. These segments range from a few hours to a week or more. The tour takes you to seven national parks, twelve national monuments, and assorted state parks, national forests, and BLM scenic areas. You'll also visit the lands of the Pueblo, Hopi, Zuñi, and Navajo people, as well as two of America's most unusual—even improbable —cities, Santa Fe and Las Vegas.

The itinerary strikes a balance between the region's famous, often crowded tourist meccas and more serene places where sightseers rarely venture. For example, you can join the throng ogling the Grand Canyon from the lodge patio; but, in case solitude suits your personal travel style better, I'll also share my own secret spot where you can camp in privacy right on the Grand Canyon rim, no ranger on duty, for free.

The itinerary format in this book is divided into 22 daily sections, containing:

1. A **suggested schedule** for each day's travel and sightseeing.

2. A detailed **travel route** description for each driving segment of your trip.

3. **Descriptive overviews** and **sightseeing highlights** (rated in order of importance: ▲▲▲ Don't miss; ▲▲ Try hard to see; and ▲ See if you get a chance).

4. A **suggested campground** for each night of the trip, as well as **restaurant and lodging recommendations** for those who choose not to camp.

5. **Helpful hints**—random tidbits that will help make your trip go well.

6. **Itinerary options**—excursion suggestions for travelers who have extra time.

7. User-friendly **maps** designed to show you what the road up ahead is really like.

Why 22 Days?

"22 Days" itinerary guidebooks like this one started in 1985 with Rick Steves's *Europe in 22 Days* (now *2 to 22 Days in Europe*), a do-it-yourself alternative to organized three-week bus tours. The series now includes such diverse destinations as Mexico, Australia, and India. You wouldn't dream of touring Europe or India in less than three weeks, because you may only have that single chance to experience what you'll remember for the rest of your life.

I invite you to explore America with the same "once in a lifetime" enthusiasm. You can see the Southwest in three weeks, for just slightly more money than you'd spend if you stayed home, and the experience will rival any foreign vacation.

Recently I commented to a ranger on the surprising number of European tourists visiting the national park where he worked. "You bet," he agreed. "Frenchmen know a lot more about this part of the country than most Americans do."

My experience verified this as I recalled working my way through college as a Pikes Peak tour guide. Every week, tourists from east of the Mississippi, where states are smaller, would tell me their trip plans: go up Pikes Peak this morning, drive on and see the Grand Canyon this afternoon, spend the night in Vegas (tomorrow it's on to Disneyland). Twelve Hours in the American Southwest. Maybe some of them accomplished it, too, back when many western highways had no speed limits. It's just that they didn't see very much.

The Southwest is vast. Distance isolates. The isolation protects ancient Native American traditions and Spanish colonial heritage. Some parts of the region remain completely uninhabited. There are roadless areas larger than some eastern states. The same vastness that makes the Southwest so alluring can isolate you behind a windshield, watching those green and white interstate signs that all look the same from coast to coast—except that out here they beckon to strange-sounding places like "Ácoma Sky City," "Shungopavi," and "Zyzyx Road." The heartland of the American Southwest ranks among the most wild and exotic places on earth. Take time to explore!

You don't even need a passport.

How Much Will It Cost?

I've taken this 22-day trip in comfort, driving a moderate-size RV with a Dodge V-8 engine, on a $1,000 trip budget, returning home with eight new pieces of Indian jewelry and twenty-one dollars in cash.

The major expense of the trip is gasoline. Figure 3,000 miles plus the round-trip driving distance from your home to the most convenient point on the tour route, at however many miles per gallon your rig gets.

If you cook your own meals, they'll cost the same as you'd spend eating at home. If you prefer the convenience of eating out, allow $5 per person per meal. There are only six towns on this 22-day trip where you can find a more expensive restaurant if you want one.

I have tried to include lodging suggestions in all price ranges when possible. In some places along this route, there are no budget motels; in other places, there are no expensive ones. If you plan to take this trip without ever camping out, budget $40 to $50 per night for lodging.

Public campground fees average $7 to $8 per night. National forests and Arizona and New Mexico state parks charge $7; Utah state parks charge $8. Most national parks and monuments charge $5 to camp, plus the admission charge. There are also abundant possibilities for free camping.

Admission to state parks, national monuments, and national parks is typically $5 per vehicle. An annual Golden Eagle Pass, admitting you to all U.S. national parks and monuments free, is a sound investment on this trip.

Souvenirs, particularly Native American arts and crafts, will tempt you to spend whatever is left of your vacation budget. I suggest that you go ahead and spend it among the Indians. Otherwise, the casino operators of Las Vegas will be waiting for you, and those guys are professionals at the art of separating tourists from their money.

When to Go

The best season for sightseeing in the Southwest is between May 1 and October 15. Before Memorial Day or after Labor Day, you can avoid crowds and extreme heat. Late spring travel reveals the desert in full bloom, while early autumn paints the mountainsides in aspen gold. However, summer travel gives you more hours of day-light, extra time to enjoy the desert at sunset and in the early morning.

Some destinations in this book, including the Grand Canyon North Rim, close in the winter. Most camp-grounds are also closed. Sudden snowstorms can inter-rupt your trip at any point. Yet winter sports enthusiasts will discover fine ski slopes with remarkably short lift lines as well as excellent cross-country ski trails and plenty of sunshine.

Other places in the Southwest, such as Phoenix,

Tucson, and the Sonora Desert are left out of the 22-day itinerary simply because they're too hot to even consider visiting in the summer months. In winter, though, these areas are warm, dry, and pleasant.

The only impossibly hot place I've included in this itinerary is the Lower Colorado River area, from Las Vegas and Lake Mead down to Lake Havasu City. You can beat the midday 100° heat with indoor sightseeing in Las Vegas and Laughlin, or with a trip to the beach.

Transportation

Seeing the Southwest by train and bus is possible and enjoyable but restricting. You can only get to the majority of places in this book by private vehicle.

I recommend a camper truck, van conversion, or small motor home for this trip, but a sporty convertible or a station wagon full of kids will do fine. You won't need four-wheel drive, though you will sometimes find yourself driving on well-maintained unpaved roads. I've included only those roads where I've personally seen large RVs go. If you have a motor home the size of a Greyhound bus, you'll need a bit of hubris but not the AAA tow truck.

Whatever vehicle you drive, be sure that it's sound enough to purr along through 3,000 miles of varied driving conditions including hot temperatures, high altitudes, and steep grades—or at least that you're equipped to handle roadside breakdowns when the nearest telephone or service station is 60 miles away. Be sure the spare tire and jack are in good condition, and carry a gallon of radiator coolant. For the confidence that comes from being ready for anything, take spare V-belts and radiator hoses as well as a basic automotive tool kit and an automotive repair manual.

RV Rentals

A growing number of visitors to the Southwest, notably European tourists, choose to fly into a western hub city like Albuquerque or Phoenix, then rent a motor home to explore more remote places where public transportation can't take them.

Many motor home dealers also act as rental agencies, representing owners who want to rent out their RVs when they're not using them, or call CruiseAmerica, (800) 327-7778, for nationwide round-trip and one-way RV rental information. In Albuquerque, Bob Myers RV Center, 12024 Central Avenue SE, (800) 748-2078, rents RVs. Rental rates vary widely, from $275 to $500 per week for van-length RVs and from $500 to $800 per week for big motor homes. It pays to shop around.

Renting an RV will cost more than all other expenses of your southwestern trip combined. If tight-budget travel is your plan, buy a tent instead. However, the luxury and comfort of motor home adventuring will cost no more than a student-style tour of Europe. It's particularly worth the extra cost if you're a newcomer to the world of RV travel and want to try one out on an extended trip before buying your own. Besides the hands-on experience, you can get ample advice about "rigs" from your neighbors in campgrounds everywhere. It's the ultimate icebreaker and a major topic of conversation.

RVs available for rent range in size from cramped to palatial. For this trip I suggest a modest size, preferably what is often called a "mini motor home," a custom-built living area mounted on a van-length frame. The places mentioned in this book can be reached even in a mammoth two-bedroom land yacht. Gas consumption will be alarming, and so will wear and tear on the driver's nerves. A big motor home is a wise choice, though, for families of four or more. It's true, you can sleep six in a mini motor home, but by Day 6 of this trip you may experience an almost overwhelming urge to leave the kids playing video games in a truck stop while you hop in your rig and high-tail it for the state line.

Food and Lodging
Tent or RV, this itinerary assumes you're equipped to camp, at least part of the time. Fine hotels and restaurants are a big industry in some southwestern communities such as Santa Fe and Las Vegas, but for more than half of

this trip, camping is the best way. On much of the route, food and lodging establishments are few, far between, and not luxurious.

My primary suggestion for each night is a public camp-ground. When possible, I've picked campgrounds where the amenities include good rest rooms, evening walking trails, and slide shows by the campfire—all for a fraction of the cost of a room with TV at a ma-and-pa highway motel.

Anyone—casual tent camper, long-term motor home traveler, or seasoned backpacker—can develop a sudden yearning for a comfortable room with a hot shower and a telephone. This book describes alternate lodging sugges-tions that range from the basic necessities to big-splurge elegance. Tenderfoot noncampers can go the whole route without sleeping outdoors. When intriguing possibilities arise—bed and breakfasts, historic hotels, national park lodges, or casino hotels—I'll give you enough details so that you can make advance reservations. Otherwise, I'll direct you to the nearest town offering reasonably priced motels.

Nearby towns are also the place to find groceries or, if you must, a cheeseburger deluxe with fries or a Mexican combination plate. Where gourmet grocery shopping or local produce is available, I'll let you know. Sometimes regional food specialties make restaurant dining a vaca-tion highlight; I'll show you the best places to find New Mexican green chile stew, Navajo fry bread, and Las Vegas bargain breakfasts as well as sunny-side up eggs overlook-ing the Grand Canyon.

Recommended Reading
2 to 22 Days in the American Southwest gives you the opportunity to see a kaleidoscope of cultures and wilder-ness panoramas. The more you know about them, the more you'll enjoy them. In this slim guide I can only tell you enough to whet your enthusiasm. Here are my favor-ite regional books, both fiction and nonfiction, available in most New Mexico and Arizona bookstores.

Charles Lummis's vivid and evocative *The Land of Poco Tiempo*, written in 1893, contains descriptions of life among the Norteño, Pueblo, and Apache people which remain surprisingly accurate nearly a century later. Also of interest is *The Delight Makers*, a novel of prehistoric Pueblo Indian life by Lummis's friend, archaeologist Adolph Bandelier.

Santa Fe's long, rich history is dramatized in a mini-Micheneresque saga entitled *The Centuries of Santa Fe* by Paul Horgan, lavish with accurate details on New Mexican life from early Spanish conquistadores to World War II. Those interested in the early years of Santa Fe's Anglo artist colony will enjoy *Artists of the Canyons and Caminos* by Edna Robertson and Sarah Nestor.

Los Alamos' Manhattan Project and its impact on neighboring communities is the subject of Frank Waters's classic *The Woman at Otowi Bridge* as well as a recent popular thriller, *Stallion Gate*, by Martin Cruz Smith.

Life in the Spanish villages of northern New Mexico is beautifully portrayed in *Bless Me, Ultima*, an autobiographical novel by University of New Mexico professor Rudolfo Anaya. For a broader, more offbeat view of the arrival of the twentieth century in northern New Mexico, read three big novels by Taos area author John Nichols: *The Milagro Beanfield War, The Magic Journey,* and *The Nirvana Blues*. The motion picture version of *The Milagro Beanfield War*, available on videocassette, may well be the best film portrayal ever of the people and problems of northern New Mexican villages.

Shelves full of books are available on the Navajo, from Navajo-English dictionaries to epic translations of Navajo song cycles. Good histories of the tribe include *The Navajo Nation* by Peter Iverson and the more readable *The Navajos* by Ruth M. Underhill. Among several accounts of traditional Navajo life told to early-twentieth-century anthropologists, my favorite is *Son of Old Man Hat*, recorded in 1934 by National Research Council Fellow Walter Dyk.

More and more mystery buffs are discovering University of New Mexico journalism professor Tony Hillerman's unique whodunits about the Navajo Tribal Police which have been hot sellers in southwestern bookstores for many years. Among them are *A Thief of Time*, *Talking God*, and *Coyote Waits*, as well as *The Dark Wind*, which producer Robert Redford recently made into a film starring Lou Diamond Phillips as Officer Jim Chee.

If I had to choose just one book for spare-time reading on this tour, it would be *Desert Solitaire*, the late Edward Abbey's memoir of a season as a ranger in Arches National Monument during the late 1950s. This collage of nature lore, environmental politics, and wilderness adventure is set in Moab, Arches, Canyonlands, Lake Powell, Capitol Reef, the Grand Canyon, and Supai. Abbey's novel, *The Monkey Wrench Gang*, a cult classic among environmental activists, inspired the popular southwestern pastime of "wrenching" (defending the environment by sabotage). Abbey's last novel, published in 1990, was a sequel to *The Monkey Wrench Gang* entitled *Hayduke Lives!*

The Exploration of the Colorado River and Its Canyons by Maj. John Wesley Powell is a record of the first expedition (1869) by river through the Grand Canyon—using wooden boats. Other enjoyable Grand Canyon classics include Joseph Wood Krutch's *Grand Canyon* and Colin Fletcher's *The Man Who Walked Through Time*.

Traveling with youngsters? John Muir Publications has recently released two Southwest guides—*Kidding Around Santa Fe* by Susan York and *Kidding Around the National Parks of the Southwest* by Sarah Lovett—designed especially for them. (But be careful. If you start reading one of these books yourself, you'll quickly discover a well-kept secret: they're not just for children!) For ordering information, see the back pages of this book.

Where to Start

2 to 22 Days in the American Southwest is a loop trip. You can start anywhere on the circle.

Albuquerque, the interstate highway system's major southwestern crossroads (I-25 north-south, I-40 east-west), is the ideal starting point for this trip if you're coming from Texas or points north or east. Albuquerque International Airport is convenient for those who plan to fly to the Southwest and then rent a vehicle.

If you're coming from the southern parts of California or Arizona, join this route on I-40 at Kingman, Arizona (Day 17), and follow the circle around (going from Day 22 to Day 1) to end your tour in Las Vegas (Day 16).

Coming from the Bay Area, northern California, or the Pacific Northwest, augment the tour by crossing the Sierras through Yosemite National Park, going south through Death Valley National Monument, starting and finishing this "22 Days" route in Las Vegas.

Interstate Alternatives

For readers with less time and those en route to someplace else, segments of this tour can be adapted as relaxing scenic alternatives to I-40, ranging from a few hours to more than a week:

■ Between Albuquerque, and Grants or Gallup, New Mexico, explore northern New Mexico, southern Colorado, and Anasazi country (Days 1 to 7).

■ Between Gallup, New Mexico, and Kingman, Arizona (also intersecting I-70 at Green River, Utah, and I-15 at St. George, Utah), travel through Hopi and Navajo reservations, Utah national parks, and Las Vegas (Days 8 to 17).

■ Between Kingman and Flagstaff, Arizona, take a scenic detour through Prescott, Jerome, and Sedona (Day 18).

■ Between Flagstaff and Holbrook, visit the Grand Canyon and Hopi mesas (Days 20 and 21).

■ Between Holbrook, Arizona, and Grants, New Mexico, visit Petrified Forest National Park, the Zuñi Reservation, El Morro, and El Malpais (Day 22).

Sightseeing highlights you can see along I-40 without major detours are those in the Albuquerque/Santa Fe area (Days 1 and 2), the Grants area (Day 6), Petrified Forest National Park (Day 7), and Flagstaff (Days 18 and 19).

In addition, travelers with limited time can abbreviate this tour into a two-week trip by jumping from Page (Day 13) to Tuba City (Day 21), an hour's drive via US 89 south and US 160 east. It's also an easy one-hour trip between Gallup (Day 8) and Grants (Day 22), a useful shortcut for splitting this itinerary into two separate trips—a New Mexico tour and an around-the-Grand Canyon tour.

The itinerary in this book is flexible. Tailor it to fit your own time frame.

Time Zones

Practically all of this tour takes place in the Rocky Mountain time zone, but during daylight saving months keeping your wristwatch correct isn't as easy as it sounds. Arizona (except for the Navajo Reservation) does not observe daylight saving time, so New Mexico and Arizona times are different in the summer, except on the Navajo Reservation, which observes daylight saving time on both sides of the state line. To keep things simple, all Suggested Schedule times in this book assume daylight saving time. If you never reset your watch, everything will work out fine.

22 Days in the American Southwest

DAY 1 In Albuquerque, New Mexico, drive or ride the aerial tramway to the top of Sandia Crest to view the land you'll be exploring during the next week. Other Albuquerque attractions include the Indian Pueblo Cultural Center and ancient petroglyphs at the edge of modern suburbs.

DAY 2 Follow the Turquoise Trail to Santa Fe, New Mexico. Spend the day visiting museums, churches, and art galleries in Santa Fe's historic plaza district as well as Indian and folk art museums.

DAY 3 En route to Bandelier National Monument, visit Shidoni's sculpture garden, San Ildefonso Pueblo, and Los Alamos. Day hike in Bandelier or explore by car higher in the Jemez Mountains.

DAY 4 Take the High Road to Taos through traditional Spanish villages, then descend into the Rio Grande Gorge. After visiting Taos, continue north into Colorado to Great Sand Dunes National Monument.

DAY 5 Play among the sand dunes. Then drive to Durango and Mesa Verde National Park. Choose either the direct route over Wolf Creek Pass or the less traveled, even more scenic route through Cumbres and Chama.

DAY 6 Visit America's largest—and most popular—cliff dwellings at Mesa Verde National Park.

DAY 7 Today's trip takes you to two other 800-year-old Anasazi cities: Aztec Ruins and isolated Chaco Canyon, the largest pueblo city ever built.

DAY 8 Return from Chaco Canyon to I-40 near Gallup, New Mexico. Drive on to the Navajo Reservation, where you'll visit the Navajo Tribal Zoo and Hubbell Trading Post, ending the day at Canyon de Chelly.

DAY 9 Travel from Canyon de Chelly to Monument Valley, with an optional detour to Navajo National Monument, site of the Anasazi cliff dwellings, Betatakin and Keet Seel. At Monument Valley Tribal Park, visit traditional Navajo homes amid landscapes familiar from cowboy movies.

DAY 10 Heading into Utah, follow the Trail of the Ancients with a morning hiking break at Natural Bridges National Monument. Continue north to the town of Moab and Canyonlands National Park's Island in the Sky.

DAY 11 Three national parks in one day: awaken in Canyonlands and get an early start to tour Arches, then drive southwest, arriving at Capitol Reef in time to enjoy the cool of the evening in Utah's least-known national park.

DAY 12 From Capitol Reef to Bryce Canyon, by way of Escalante Canyons, is one of the most beautiful stretches of road on this tour. At busy Bryce Canyon National Park, take an easy walk along the canyon rim or a more demanding one down among the hoodoos.

DAY 13 Take a scenic detour to Glen Canyon Dam and spend the night at Lee's Ferry, where the Grand Canyon begins.

DAY 14 Spend a day and night on the North Rim of the Grand Canyon.

DAY 15 Travel from the Grand Canyon through Zion National Park, then take I-15 to Las Vegas. Rather than rush into the city, why not enjoy a peaceful desert night in the Valley of Fire?

DAY 16 Bright lights, noise, glitz, greed, and fast money round the clock: experience Las Vegas. Approach the city by the scenic route along the Lake Mead shore to Hoover Dam. Swim and sunbathe at a desert beach.

DAY 17 Following the Colorado River southward, visit the riverside fishing-and-gaming community of Laugh-lin, Nevada/Bullhead City, Arizona, then see the London Bridge, improbably relocated to Lake Havasu City. In

Kingman, hike at Hualapai Mountain, an island of cool forest in the middle of the Mohave Desert.

DAY 18 Drive either I-40 or empty old Route 66 to Ash Fork, then turn south to loop through three unique central Arizona towns, each strikingly different from the others—Prescott, Jerome, and Sedona.

Day 19 Keep the same campsite or motel room. Within a few minutes' drive of the city limits, sightseeing highlights include Walnut Canyon National Monument, Lowell Observatory, and the Museum of Northern Arizona.

DAY 20 Return to the Grand Canyon, this time visiting the South Rim. On the way there, see Sunset Crater and Wupatki national monuments.

DAY 21 Drive across the desert of the western Navajo Reservation to one of the most remote places in the United States, the ancient group of villages on top of the Hopi mesas.

DAY 22 Cross I-40 at Petrified Forest National Park, with its red, white, and blue painted desert. Then drive through the Zuñi Reservation to El Morro National Monument, the nation's first. Around Grants, New Mexico, visit El Malpais National Monument and Ácoma Pueblo. You're now just a one-hour drive from Albuquerque, where this tour began three weeks ago.

ALBUQUERQUE

At the crossroads of two interstate highways and with the
state's only major commercial airport, Albuquerque is the
natural place to begin a tour of northern New Mexico and
the Four Corners area.

Before World War II, Albuquerque was a sleepy little
university town about the same size as Santa Fe. Its strate-
gic location at the intersection of I-25 and I-40 explains
why the city is approaching half a million in population,
while other New Mexican towns remain small. All streets
are designated by quadrant. For example, if you're on
Lomas Boulevard NE, you are north of Central Avenue
(old Route 66) and east of the railroad tracks. These traditional dividing lines meet close enough to the "Big I"—
the intersection of Interstates 25 and 40—so that the
quadrant system will generally tell you which direction
you are from both major freeways. It's hard to get lost as
long as you remember that Sandia Crest, the big mountain nearby, is to the east.

Suggested Schedule

10:00 a.m.	Drive to Petroglyph Park on the city's west edge.
10:30 a.m.	Walk through Petroglyph Park.
11:00 a.m.	Return to I-40 and drive to the Pueblo Cultural Center.
11:30 a.m.	Visit the Pueblo Cultural Center. Eat lunch at the restaurant there.
1:00 p.m.	Drive to the Sandia Tramway station.
1:30 p.m.	Ride the tramway to Sandia Crest.
2:00 p.m.	Hike Sandia Crest.
4:00 p.m.	Descend from the mountain.
4:30 p.m.	Visit Old Town, a good area for strolling and dining.

Sightseeing Highlights

▲▲ **Indian Petroglyph National Monument**—West Mesa Escarpment, the cliff below the small, extinct volcanoes on the horizon, defines the western edge of Albuquerque. Housing subdivisions sprawl up to the base of the escarpment; from the top rim, the land is empty and almost roadless for a hundred miles to the west, home only to jackrabbits and coyotes. The black volcanic boulders tumbled all along the escarpment contain over 15,000 pre-Columbian Indian petroglyphs—more than at any other site in the United States. Much of this rock art dates back a thousand years or more.

In 1988, the federal government decided to declare a large area of the West Mesa Escarpment a national monument, but so far the funds have not been available to develop the park. You can see some of the best rock art by climbing the trail through the part of the park where Atrisco road nears the top rim of the escarpment.

The meanings of some of the petroglyphs, such as animal pictures, are self-evident, and anthropologists have interpreted some of the abstract symbols with the help of modern-day Rio Grande Pueblo people, whose ancient ancestors chipped them into the rocks. Some of the figures remain mysterious. Notice the images of Kokopelli, the hunchbacked flute player thought to symbolize fertility, which are common throughout the Anasazi country in New Mexico, Colorado, Utah, and Arizona. Humanlike horned figures may represent prehistoric shamans. Early Spanish settlers believed that they were devils and carved crosses near them to neutralize their supposed black magic powers.

To reach Petroglyph Park, take I-40 west and turn off northbound at Coors Road, exit 155. Veer left and follow Atrisco Road to the park.

▲▲ **Indian Pueblo Cultural Center**—Owned by the Native American Pueblos of New Mexico, this cultural center has a series of galleries selling Indian arts and crafts in all price ranges surrounding the central open-air dance plaza, as well as a museum. Indian dances and craft dem-

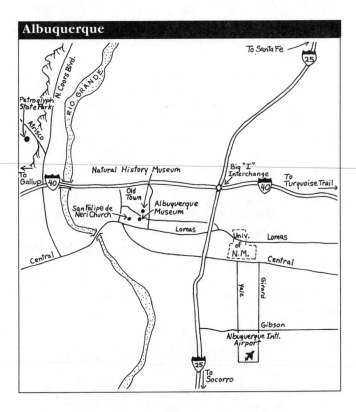

Albuquerque

onstrations are held here on most weekends during the spring, summer, and autumn months—sometimes free, other times for a small admission fee; for the current schedule of events, call (505) 843-7270. The cultural center also has a moderately priced restaurant specializing in Native American cuisine, making it an ideal lunch stop. Open daily from 9:00 a.m. to 5:30 p.m., closed Thanksgiving, Christmas, and New Year's Day. Admission to the retail galleries is free; entry to the museum costs $2.50 for adults, $1.50 for seniors over age 62, $1 for school-age children. The center is at 2401 12th Street NW, a few blocks north of I-40 exit 157B.

▲▲▲ **Sandia Crest**—A trip to the mountaintop is a must for visitors, not only for the spectacular view but also because temperatures on Sandia Crest average about 30 degrees cooler than downtown, offering a welcome escape from the city's midsummer afternoon heat. You can get to the summit by riding the world's longest aerial tramway or by driving the steep paved road up the back side of the mountain, a side trip from the Turquoise Trail.

To take the Sandia Peak Aerial Tramway (adults $10.50, seniors and students $8), go east on I-40 to Exit 167 and follow Tramway Boulevard north for 10 miles to the base terminal. The tramway operates daily during the summer months from 9:00 a.m. to 10:00 p.m., and during spring and autumn daily from 9:00 a.m. to 9:00 p.m. except Wednesday, when it does not begin running until 5:00 p.m.; closed during ski season.

To drive to the top of Sandia Crest and see the view for free, follow the Turquoise Trail (see Day 2). The steep, paved road up to Sandia Crest splits off to the left at Cedar Crest, the first town you reach on NM 14 after leaving the interstate.

An easy, mile-long walking trail along the crest between the tramway station and the auto road summit house gives you an eagle's-eye view of the city a mile below. There is a snack bar at the auto road summit house and a more complete restaurant and bar at the tramway station. The crest trail continues in both directions for a total distance of more than twenty miles.

Your itinerary for the next week lies before your eyes as you survey the 360-degree horizon from Sandia Crest. To the north, bordering the Rio Grande, the volcanic Jemez Mountains conceal Los Alamos and Bandelier National Monument (Day 3). The Sangre de Cristo Mountains to the northeast range from Santa Fe at the southern tip in a nearly unbroken wall of rock for 200 miles north past Taos into Colorado and beyond the Great Sand Dunes (Day 4). Far on the northern skyline, you may barely make out southwestern Colorado's San Juan Mountains, which you'll cross on your way west to Durango and Mesa Verde (Day 5). Then you'll return south through Chaco Canyon (Day 7) in the San Juan Basin, which lies

between the Jemez Mountains and Mt. Taylor, the big soli-
tary mountain that should be clearly visible to the west.
South of Mt. Taylor are Ácoma, El Malpais, and El Morro
(Day 22). Beyond Mt. Taylor is Navajo country.

"Sandia," by the way, means "watermelon" in Spanish.

▲▲ **Old Town**—Albuquerque's original town plaza, dating back to 1706, has remained remarkably intact as high-
rise buildings have sprouted up all around it in recent
years, creating an oasis of antiquity in the midst of the
modern city. Browse in the art galleries and shops; exam-
ine the wares of the Pueblo Indian vendors who line the
sidewalks. Pause for a quiet moment in the eighteenth-
century San Felipe de Neri Church on the northwest corner of the plaza. Free walking tours of Old Town start
from the nearby Albuquerque Museum, 2000 Mountain
Road NW, 243-7255, Wednesday through Friday at 11:00
a.m., Saturday and Sunday at 1:30 p.m. Old Town is one-
half mile south of I-40 exit 157A via Rio Grande
Boulevard.

▲ **Albuquerque's Museums**—You will have a chance
to visit several of the Southwest's finest museums tomorrow in Santa Fe, but for serious museum buffs as well as
visitors who find themselves in Albuquerque on an unlikely rainy day and want to do their sightseeing indoors,
here is an array of first-rate possibilities.

The New Mexico Museum of Natural History contains
full-scale dinosaur models, exhibits about New Mexico's
human and animal inhabitants in the last Ice Age, and a
large display about the Rio Grande including aquariums
of fish that live in the river. The most unusual and
memorable of the museum's exhibits is a quite realistic
simulation of a journey into the depths of a volcano.
Open daily from 9:00 a.m. to 5:00 p.m., adults $4, stu-
dents and senior citizens $3, children ages 3 to 11 $1. The
museum is at 1801 Mountain Road NW, near Old Town.
For current exhibit information, call 841-8837.

Across the road, the Albuquerque Museum features an
impressive permanent exhibit entitled Four Centuries: A
History of Albuquerque, containing the largest collec-

tion of Spanish colonial artifacts in the United States. The museum is open daily except Monday from 9:00 a.m. to 5:00 p.m. Admission is free.

The Maxwell Museum of Anthropology on the University of New Mexico campus contains exhibits on the Athabascan (Navajo and Apache) and Anasazi cultures, with special emphasis on Chaco Canyon, and provides a good introduction to many Native American tribes and sites you will see later in this itinerary. The university is about 2 miles east of I-25 via Central Avenue; Maxwell Museum is near the west edge of the campus, two blocks north of Central on Redondo Drive. Open Monday through Friday from 9:00 a.m. to 4:00 p.m., Saturday from 10:00 a.m. to 4:00 p.m., closed Sunday, free. Phone 277-4404 for information.

The Spanish History Museum displays the colonial history of New Mexico from the travels of early conquistadores to 1912, when statehood was granted. Other exhibits reveal the roles Hispanics have played in U.S. history, such as Spanish aid to George Washington's revolutionary army. The museum is two blocks south of the University of New Mexico at 2221 Lead SE. Open daily 1:00 to 5:00 p.m. Admission is $1 per person, children under 5 free. Phone 268-9981 for information.

Camping

The most convenient public campground in the Albuquerque area is at **Coronado State Monument**, 15 minutes north of the city on I-25. Campsites, which cost $9, are along the Rio Grande riverbank. Pueblo ruins at the monument feature a kiva with rare restored wall murals.

Several private RV campgrounds with full hookups are located near I-40 at the western edge of the city. Try the **Albuquerque West KOA,** not far from Petroglyph Park, at 5739 Ouray Road NW one-half mile north of the Coors Road exit from I-40, (505) 831-1991. Mesa-top campsites cost $15.

Lodging

For luxury accommodations in a historic hotel, Albuquerque's best is **La Posada de Albuquerque**, downtown at 125 Second Street (corner of Copper), (505) 242-9090, or, from outside New Mexico, (800) 621-7231. This was the first hotel ever built by New Mexico native Conrad Hilton. (It is no longer affiliated with the Hilton chain.) While the building only dates back to 1939, its lavish 1984 restoration has given it a distinctly Victorian air with classic New Mexican touches. Room rates range from $78 to $102 double.

Perhaps Albuquerque's most unique bed and breakfast is **Casas de Sueños**, 310 Rio Grande SW, (505) 247-4560. The compound of casitas in a garden setting, two blocks from Old Town Plaza and across the street from the country club golf course, was originally the home of painter/photographer J. R. Willis, best known for Indian postcards sold along Route 66 in the 1940s which are now valuable collectors' items. An addition to the main house, published in many professional journals, launched the career of world-renowned architect Bart Prince, who recently designed the Oriental addition to the Los Angeles County Art museum. Room rates at Casas de Sueños start at $70 a night and go all the way up to $250 for a two-bedroom private house.

Another great Albuquerque bed-and-breakfast inn is the **William E. Mauger Estate**, near Old Town at 701 Roma Avenue NW, (505) 242-8755. This three-story brick Queen Anne Victorian mansion, built in 1896, has eight guest rooms with antique furnishings and private baths. Room rates of $50 to $75 double include continental breakfast. Reservations are essential.

Name-brand motor hotels cluster around the intersection of I-25 and Lomas Boulevard, including the **Holiday Inn-Midtown**, 2020 Menaul Boulevard NE, (505) 884-2511, doubles $79 and up, and the **Albuquerque Hilton**, 1901 University Boulevard NE, (505) 884-2500, doubles from $85. Farther north on I-25 is the **Holiday Inn Journal Center**, 5151 San Francisco Road NE (at exit

232), (505) 821-3333. Built in the shape of an Aztec pyramid, this hotel has a fifty-foot waterfall inside its ten-story atrium lobby. Rates are $92 to $102 double. Catering primarily to businessmen, several of these hotels offer special rates on weekend nights.

Good budget bets include the **Lorilodge Motel East** at 801 Central Avenue NE, just off I-25, (505) 243-2891, with doubles from $22 to $30, and the **De Anza Motel**, 4301 Central Avenue NE, (505) 255-1654, with doubles for under $30.

Food

The best bet for lunch is the restaurant at the **Indian Pueblo Cultural Center** (see Sightseeing Highlights), open daily from 7:30 a.m. to 3:30 p.m. Specialties are Native American dishes such as Indian tacos, posole, and spiced bread pudding.

High on Sandia Crest, with prices to match, **High Finance** at the top of the tramway serves steaks, seafood, pasta, and Mexican food daily from 11:00 a.m. to 2:30 p.m. and 4:30 to 9:00 p.m., with barbecues on weekends. Sunset dining here makes for an incomparable experience. Guests with dinner reservations receive a discount on tram ticket prices.

Another extraordinary luxury restaurant is the **Ranchers Club** in the Albuquerque Hilton hotel, 1901 University Avenue NE, 884-2500. As the name suggests, steak is the specialty here—but no ordinary steak. The menu includes a 40-ounce T-bone and a 48-ounce porterhouse. Guests can choose which wood will be used to barbecue their steaks—mesquite, hickory, sassafras, or wild cherry.

Good places to dine around Old Town include **Maria Teresa**, 618 Rio Grande Boulevard, 242-3900, and **High Noon**, 425 San Felipe NW, 765-1455; both are in historic buildings and both specialize in New Mexican and Continental cuisine. For more moderate prices on Old Town Plaza, enjoy Mexican food at colorful **La Hacienda**, 243-3131, serving from 11:00 a.m. to 9:00 p.m. daily. A

still more affordable restaurant in the same area, for lunch
only, is **Christopher's**, 323 Romero NW, 242-0202, serving New Mexican food daily from 11:00 a.m. to 3:00 p.m.

For low-priced eating with the college crowd, especially recommended for breakfast, try the huevos ran-
cheros (fried eggs on a tortilla, smothered in hot salsa)
and giant cinnamon rolls at the **Frontier** on Central Avenue across from the University of New Mexico campus,
open daily from 6:30 a.m. to midnight.

Another unique, budget-priced restaurant in the university area is the **66 Diner**, 1405 Central Avenue NE,
247-1421, a 1950s-style diner that enthusiastically pro-
motes nostalgia for old Route 66, which ran through
Albuquerque on Central Avenue before Interstate 40 was
built. The chef recommends the fries, shakes, and green
chile cheese dogs.

Nightlife

The University of New Mexico is the hub of Albuquerque's active performing arts sphere. On campus, **Pope-
joy Hall** (277-3824) hosts the Albuquerque Civic Light
Opera, the New Mexico Jazz Workshop, and the New
Mexico Symphony Orchestra, as well as popular music
concerts. The historic **KiMo Theater**, downtown at 423
Central Avenue NE, 848-1370, is the venue for performances by such groups as the Albuquerque Ballet Company, the New Mexico Repertory Company, and the
unique Compania de Teatro, a repertory group that per-
forms plays in English, Spanish, and even Northern New
Mexican "Spanglish."

The top student hangout in the university district is the
Fat Chance Bar and Grille, 216 Central Avenue SE,
296-5653, featuring food, drinks, amiable crowds, and
loud live music. Country fans, head for the **Sundance
Saloon & Dance Hall**, 12000 Candelaria Boulevard NE,
296-6761, where top C&W bands perform nightly. Dance
lessons are available on weeknights. Albuquerque's big
comedy club is Laffs, 3100 Juan Tabo Boulevard NE,
296-5653. Tuesdays are open-mike amateur nights.

Hot Air Balloons

You can't go far in Albuquerque without seeing the ubiq-
uitous hot air balloon motif that is this city's claim to
fame. The **Albuquerque Balloon Fiesta**, held annually
in early October, is the largest event of its kind in the
world, featuring mass ascensions of over 500 balloons
and drawing crowds of over half a million. If the Balloon
Fiesta doesn't fit into your trip schedule, you can still see
anywhere from a dozen to fifty balloons floating above
the city, roaring with sounds like dragon breath and
sometimes bouncing off suburban rooftops, practically
any sunny weekend morning. The best spot from which
to watch this spectacle is the rim of West Mesa Escarpment, reached via the maze of unpaved roads to the
south above Petroglyph National Monument.

DAY 2
SANTA FE

From Albuquerque, a one-hour drive will take you across the stretch of rugged mountains and high desert to the gateway of one of our nation's most isolated corners, where history has created a tricultural blend that is unique in the world. Santa Fe has been New Mexico's capital since A.D. 1610.

Northern New Mexico feels foreign, and it's no wonder. For over two centuries, New Mexico was the northernmost Spanish colony in the New World, its border closed to foreigners. It became a state of newly independent Mexico in 1821 but was demoted to Mexican territorial status in 1836, invaded by the Republic of Texas in 1841, occupied by the U.S. Army in 1846 during the Mexican War, declared U.S. territory in 1848, and unsuccessfully invaded by the Confederacy in 1862. It became a U.S. state in 1912. Which nation owns New Mexico at the moment is of little import to local residents, who know their home is unlike anyplace else in America.

Suggested Schedule

9:00 a.m.	Drive the Turquoise Trail to Santa Fe.
10:30 a.m.	Stroll Santa Fe Plaza. See the Palace of the Governors, the New Mexico Fine Arts Museum, and art galleries.
1:00 p.m.	Green chile for lunch.
2:00 p.m.	Visit the Folk Art and Indian Arts museums or take an afternoon drive to Pecos.
Evening	Dinner and nightlife.

Travel Route: Albuquerque to Santa Fe (69 miles)
Drive the Turquoise Trail (NM 14) from Albuquerque to Santa Fe. It takes just 15 minutes longer than I-25 North and is a calmer, prettier drive. From the "Big I" (where I-40 intersects I-25) in Albuquerque, take I-40 East 15

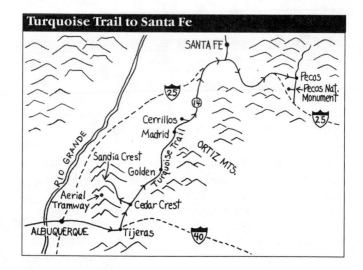

Turquoise Trail to Santa Fe

miles to exit 175 (Tijeras, Cedar Crest) and turn north (left) from the off-ramp.

The route takes you over the small but rugged Ortiz Range, site of the first gold discovery in what's now the United States. The former coal mining town of Madrid, once nearly abandoned and now revived by artists and refugees from modern living, has a mining museum with an underground tour, as well as one of the Santa Fe area's livelier live music night spots, the Mine Shaft Tavern.

Cerrillos, an off-the-beaten-path village with few concessions to tourism (or to the twentieth century) is worth a short stop and stroll. Follow the signs through town to the edge of the arroyo and visit Casa Grande, (505) 471-2744, an old 20-room adobe compound converted into a delightfully down-home bed and breakfast, petting zoo, and private museum of locally gathered turquoise, artifacts, and antique arroyo junk. If you have extra time, inquire at Casa Grande to arrange a personal four-wheel-drive and hiking tour of the old Pueblo Indian turquoise mines in the hills nearby.

If you have extra time to explore, detour south instead of north when you reach I-25 and visit El Rancho de las Golondrinas (exit 271 and follow the "Golondrinas

Museum" signs). This well-preserved Spanish Colonial hacienda, circa 1710, was an important rest stop on the Camino Real from Mexico City. It is open for self-guided tours during the summer months—Wednesday through Sunday from 10:00 a.m. to 4:00 p.m.; adults $3, students 13 to 18 $2, children 5 to 12 $1. Several miles of walking trails afford tranquillity, and visitors are few except during Harvest Festival in early October, coinciding with the Albuquerque Balloon Fiesta, when costumed volunteers re-create the colonial era.

When you reach I-25, don't continue into Santa Fe on NM 14 unless you're looking for a moderately priced motel. The highway becomes Cerrillos Road, a congested 6-mile strip that is Santa Fe's "other side of the tracks." Instead, take I-25 northbound for 6 miles to the Old Pecos Trail exit for a more attractive approach to downtown Santa Fe.

Free Parking Downtown: When you cross the Santa Fe River, you're within walking distance of the plaza. Look for a parking spot along the river on Alameda between Paseo de Peralta and Delgado Street. Walk one long block north on Paseo de Peralta to Palace Avenue, then three blocks east to the plaza. If you can't find parking on Alameda, turn around and follow Paseo de Peralta north to the intersection with Washington Street (by the big pink Moorish-style Masonic Temple) and turn right, then right again onto Artist Road (follow the Hyde Park/Ski Basin signs), and just above the Fort Marcy condominium complex turn right again onto Prince Street. Park anywhere along this street and walk across the mesa-top park to the tall white Cross of the Martyrs for a view of downtown, then descend the brick-cobbled walkway. Walk 1½ blocks south (left) on Paseo de Peralta to Palace Avenue and three blocks west (right) to the plaza.

Santa Fe

Santa Fe (pop. 60,000) prides itself on its antiquity and blend of Native American, Hispanic, and Anglo cultural influences. The Pueblo people have occupied the area for

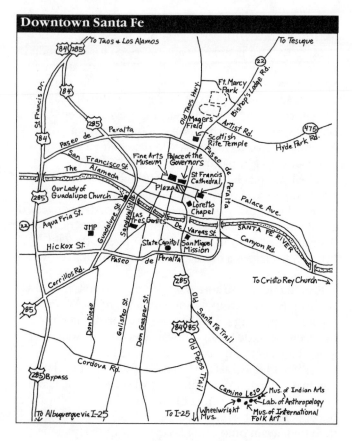

Downtown Santa Fe

at least 700 years, while the Hispanics arrived almost 400 years ago to establish the northernmost Spanish colony in the New World. Santa Fe's population today is about 60 percent Hispanic, and a distinctive regional dialect of Spanish is commonly spoken. The capital of a culturally diverse state that also has Texas-style cattle ranching east of the mountains, the Navajo Nation in the west, and the Mexican border to the south, Santa Fe is a southwestern microcosm.

Among Santa Fe's most noticeable characteristics is adobe architecture. The Spanish Pueblo style, with protruding vigas (roof beams), is an adaptation of the Middle

Eastern architecture brought to Spain by the Moors and to New Mexico by the Spanish, then influenced by Pueblo Indian construction techniques. The territorial style, with red bricks along the roofline, developed in the late nineteenth century with the introduction of building materials from the United States.

The city's Historic Styles Act, passed in 1957, requires that all new construction in the downtown historic district be Spanish Pueblo or territorial in appearance, even though modern building methods and materials may be used. The law also limits building height and window space and prohibits large or electrified signs. The result, a low-rise earth-tone city center preserving an Old World feel, is easy on the eyes.

Though museums and churches provide a framework for sightseeing, Santa Fe is a shopper's town, where Native American artifacts and traditional crafts, traditional western paintings, and contemporary Indian and non-Indian works of art, as well as aggressively regional Santa Fe-style "wearable art" fashions, are displayed in bewildering profusion. Quality is exceptional, with prices to match. Are you in the market for a painting that costs more than a car? If not, just browsing in the plaza area and Canyon Road galleries can introduce you to the visual glories of the American Southwest through the eyes of its best artists.

Santa Fe Downtown Walking Tour

One block east of the plaza or town square, on the north side of Palace Avenue, is Sena Plaza, a former Spanish colonial mansion whose interior courtyard provides a quiet, cool sitting spot. From there, proceed to the center of the plaza, where a monument commemorates Santa Feans' valor in repelling various nineteenth-century invaders such as Confederate troops and [   ] Indians. (The eradicated word was "savage." Locals hasten to point out that these weren't local Indians but rather Comanches who came from Texas—as, for that matter, did the Confederate soldiers.) Facing the plaza on the north side is the

Palace of the Governors, housing the New Mexico
Museum of History, a must-see for anyone interested in
the region's Spanish colonial heritage. The next block
west of the Palace is the New Mexico Fine Arts Museum.
Allow at least two hours to see both museums.

When you exit the art museum, walk diagonally across
the plaza to La Fonda, Santa Fe's oldest hotel. Browse
through the hotel's lobby, interesting for its unusual
decor, then exit and continue west up San Francisco
Street to St. Francis Cathedral. Return from the cathedral
to La Fonda and turn left (south) down Old Santa Fe Trail
one block to Loretto Chapel on the grounds of the Inn at
Loretto. On the same street, across the river, are San
Miguel Mission and the Oldest House. Continue about
two more blocks in the same direction on Old Santa Fe
Trail to the New Mexico State Capitol Building, then backtrack to the plaza. At some point along this suggested
tour, you'll probably be distracted by art galleries and
shops. Wander and browse—you can't go wrong.

Santa Fe Sightseeing Highlights
**▲▲▲ Palace of the Governors (New Mexico
Museum of History)**—This is the oldest public building
in the United States, dating back to 1610. Emphasis is on
the colonial and territorial eras. Permanent exhibits include photographic reproductions of Spanish colonial
maps of the Southwest as well as a beautiful full-scale
reconstruction of a Penitente chapel. Open daily from
10:00 a.m. to 5:00 p.m., closed Mondays off-season.
Admission is $3.50 for adults, under 16 years old free. A
two-day pass for admission to the Palace of the Governors, Fine Arts Museum, International Museum of Folk
Art, and Museum of Indian Arts and Culture (in tomorrow's listings) costs only $6 and saves you $8 per person.

Indians selling jewelry and pottery at the Palace of the
Governors portico enjoy official status as an "exhibit" of
the Museum of New Mexico, which regulates the quality
and authenticity of their goods.

▲▲▲ **New Mexico Fine Arts Museum**—Built in 1917 to encourage Santa Fe's burgeoning artist colony, the museum with its stylized neo-Spanish Pueblo look sparked a resurgence of the architecture that character-izes Santa Fe today. The museum formerly provided dis-play space for local artists as well as a framing workshop in the basement and free monthly banquets upstairs. In those days, Santa Fe's artist population was small enough to fit in one room. Today the upstairs galleries house clas-sic paintings from early-twentieth-century Santa Fe and Taos. The main floor galleries rotate exhibits with empha-sis on contemporary New Mexican artists. St. Francis Auditorium, adjoining the museum, is patterned on a grand scale after the interiors of early New Mexican mis-sion churches, with a series of frescoes depicting Francis-can missionary history. The museum is open daily from 10:00 a.m. to 5:00 p.m., closed Mondays off-season. Admission $3.50 for adults, free under age 16.

▲▲▲ **IAIA Museum**—Operated by the federal govern-ment, the Institute of American Indian Arts in Santa Fe provides free training for the most talented young Indian artists from all over the United States. Its presence has been a major factor in the emergence of Santa Fe as the largest market for contemporary Native American art. The new museum, a converted former federal office building that opened in downtown Santa Fe in June 1992, features "Creativity is Our Tradition: Three Decades of Contemporary Art at the IAIA," as well as changing spe-cial exhibitions, a performance gallery, and a museum shop featuring exceptional contemporary Indian art works.The museum is open Monday through Saturday from 9:00 a.m. to 6:00 p.m. (8:00 p.m. on Wednesdays) and Sunday from 12:00 noon to 6:00 p.m. during the summer months, Monday through Friday from 10:00 a.m. to 5:00 p.m. and Saturday and Sunday from 12:00 noon to 5:00 p.m. the rest of the year. Admission is $3.50 for adults, $2.00 for senior citizens, students with I.D., and children under age 16.

▲▲ **St. Francis Cathedral**—This church was built in 1869 by Archbishop Jean Baptiste Lamy, the French cler-gyman who was transferred here from Cleveland, Ohio, to restore mainstream Catholicism to New Mexico. (The Mexican government had banished all Spanish-born priests 41 years before. In isolation from the mother church, spiritual needs were served by the Brothers of Light, a lay Penitente sect that remains alive and well in rural New Mexico. After U.S. occupation, both the Catholic church and the federal government feared the Brotherhood's influence.) The cathedral's most notable feature is La Conquistadora, housed to the left of the altar in a chapel that was part of the original church on this site. The blue-clad willow wood statue of the Virgin, carried by Spanish refugees in their flight from the Pueblo Revolt of 1680, is the oldest surviving religious carving in New Mexico and the centerpiece of a thanksgiving procession (during Fiesta, the weekend after Labor Day) that has been held annually since 1716.

▲ **Loretto Chapel (Chapel of Our Lady of Light)**— Another Archbishop Lamy creation, the chapel is best known for its "miraculous staircase." Legend has it that the architect abandoned the project (some say he was caught with the bishop's nephew's wife) without building any stairs to the choir loft. A Mysterious Carpenter (the faithful believe he was St. Joseph, though skeptical historians claim he was an Austrian tourist) appeared and built this beautiful curved staircase without using any nails. Then he vanished without asking for payment. (Say, that *is* mysterious. . . .) Open daily from 9:00 a.m. to 5:00 p.m., admission 50 cents donation.

▲ **San Miguel Mission**—This chapel, claimed to be the Oldest Church in the United States, was built in 1710 on the rubble of a 1626 mission church destroyed during the Pueblo Revolt. Two other early mission churches still stand—at Ácoma (1629), which you'll see on Day 22, and at Isleta (1630)—so whether this one really counts as the oldest church is a matter of controversy. It's old, though, and reveals the spiritual side of Spanish colonial life.

Indian relics are on display from the centuries-old pueblo that was demolished to build the earlier church. Open Monday through Saturday from 9:00 a.m. to 4:30 p.m. and Sundays from 1:00 to 4:30 p.m. Donations are accepted. There is a Catholic curio shop.

▲ **State Capitol**—A big circular flat-roofed neoterritorial style building, the "Roundhouse" looks nothing like a capitol building is supposed to. Its floor plan was patterned after the Zia Pueblo sun symbol that graces the New Mexico flag and license plates. Stroll through the gardens, landscaped with vegetation from all parts of New Mexico, and the newly renovated rotunda. A former state capitol, still the prettiest building in the state government complex, is the nearby Bataan Building, whose classic dome was removed in 1951. Open Monday through Friday from 8:00 a.m. to 5:00 p.m. and on Saturdays during the summer months from 9:00 a.m. to 4:00 p.m.

▲▲ **Canyon Road**—Drive up Canyon Road, the first left turn off Paseo de Peralta after you cross the river heading south, to see the original center of Santa Fe's artist colony, now a mixed bag of small studio/galleries and more commercial restaurants and shops. If Santa Fe's art scene has sparked an urge in you to take up sketching again (you'll find plenty of inspiration in the coming weeks), the Artisan on Canyon Road is among the most complete art supply stores you're ever likely to find.

Where Canyon Road stops being one way, turn right on Camino del Monte Sol and drive south to Old Santa Fe Trail. Take a one-block jog to your right (downhill) to Camino Lejo, with its big "Museums" sign, and turn there to find the following three museums where you can spend the whole morning and wish you had more time.

▲▲ **New Mexico Museum of Indian Arts and Culture** —This outstanding museum presents selections from the state of New Mexico's 50,000 Indian artifacts, with Native American participation in exhibit planning, and works from the Institute of American Indian Art. One exhibit shows aerial photographs of Pueblo ruins that non-Indians cannot visit in person, including the ancient pueblo on Black Mesa above San Ildefonso Pueblo (Day 3). There are often craft demonstrations. The gift shop has an excellent selection of books on Indian subjects. Open daily from 10:00 a.m. to 5:00 p.m., closed Mondays off-season; admission $3.50 for adults, free under age 16.

▲▲▲ **New Mexico Museum of International Folk Art**—Among the most unusual museums anywhere, this is the place in Santa Fe to take children if you have any along. It can also bring out the childlike wonder in you. Amble through the Spanish colonial and other folk art exhibits to the Girard Wing, where you'll find a phenomenal collection of handcrafted toys and miniatures from throughout the world arranged in enchanting dioramas. The museum's gift shop is wonderful. Open daily from 10:00 a.m. to 5:00 p.m., closed Mondays off-season. Admission is $3.50 for adults, free under age 16.

▲▲▲ **Wheelwright Museum of American Indian Art**—This small private museum features rotating traditional and modern Native American art exhibits. It was founded, with guidance from famed Navajo shaman Hosteen Klah, by Mary Wheelwright, daughter of an aristocratic Bostonian family who came west to live among the Indians. The building is in the eight-sided hogan shape that Navajo ceremonies require. Downstairs, Case Trading Post sells Native American arts and crafts of assured quality in all price ranges as well as books, posters, and handmade cards. Open Monday through Saturday from 10:00 a.m. to 5:00 p.m. and Sundays from 1:00 to 5:00 p.m. Donations welcome.

▲ **Randall Davey Audubon Center**—If you'd rather be outdoors, make time in your morning schedule to visit the estate of a longtime Santa Fe artist who left his home and 135-acre grounds to the National Audubon Society as a wildlife refuge. At the mouth of Santa Fe Canyon (a municipal watershed that has been closed to the public for 50 years), wildlife that sometimes wanders down to these meadows includes coyotes, raccoons, black bears, mountain lions, bobcats, and mule deer. The refuge is home to over 100 species of birds and 120 species of plants. The grounds are open daily from 9:00 a.m. to 5:00 p.m. A $1 admission fee is requested from non-Audubon members. Call (505) 983-4609 for information on guided history tours of the Randall Davey house.

To get there, take Canyon Road as far as it goes. When it seems to end, jog one block to the right, then left onto Upper Canyon Road. The Randall Davey Center is as far up Upper Canyon Road as you're allowed to drive.

Camping

A good camping area near Santa Fe is the National Forest **Black Canyon Campground** ($7 sites) or adjoining **Hyde Memorial State Park** ($9 sites), both 7 miles up Hyde Park-Ski Basin Road from downtown (take Washington Street north from downtown and turn right at the sign). If you decide to stay in town late for nightlife and after-hours window-shopping, camping spots will still be available at Hyde Park, a popular picnic area where sites are often occupied until late in the afternoon by day users. Overnight parking is also allowed 10 miles farther up the road at the Ski Basin parking area, a major Pecos Wilderness trailhead with picnic tables and rest rooms.

Hyde Park is nearly 9,000 feet in altitude, compared with 5,000 feet in Albuquerque and 7,000 feet in Santa Fe. The Ski Basin parking lot is over 10,000 feet, about the same as the summit of Sandia Crest. As you probably noticed this morning on Sandia, higher elevations mean cooler temperatures. Each 1,000 feet of altitude drops the temperature about 9 degrees F, as great a difference as traveling 300 miles north, so temperatures at Hyde Park average 35 degrees cooler than in Albuquerque, about the same as in Calgary, Alberta. Nights can be chilly at any time of year. By the way, the vehicles-prohibited maintenance road that runs 6 miles up to the 12,010-foot summit of Lake Peak from the Aspen Vista parking area midway between Hyde Park and the Ski Basin makes for lovely walking. In early October it becomes a "must-see" sight, as autumn colors brighten the largest continuous forest of aspen trees in the world.

Apache Canyon KOA is a large commercial campground with full hookups located on Old Pecos Trail, the
two-lane highway that parallels I-25 northbound from
Santa Fe. Sites cost about $16. Another campground
within easy driving distance of Santa Fe is operated by
Indians. The **Tesuque Pueblo RV Campground** is just
off US 285 next to the landmark Camel Rock, 10 miles
north of the city. Amenities include a heated swimming
pool, a hot tub, and a bingo parlor just across the highway. Nearby Tesuque Pueblo is small but picturesque.
Sites cost about $15.

Lodging

Choosing to stay in town rather than camping tonight will
give you a better chance to enjoy evening entertainment.
Most downtown hotels are luxurious and costly.

My favorite Santa Fe luxury hotel is the new **Hotel
Santa Fe**, 1501 Paseo de Peralta at Cerrillos Road, (505)
982-1200 or (800) 825-9876. This exceptionally comfortable Pueblo Revival-style hotel, decorated with native
American art including numerous bronze works by
famed Apache sculptor Allan Houser, is unique in that it is
51 percent owned by an Indian pueblo. The federal government makes economic development funds available
to Indian tribes under the Indian Financing Act of 1974,
and these funds are usually used to start businesses—
from bingo parlors to chopstick factories—on the reservations. But tiny Picurís Pueblo, hidden deep in the
Sangre de Cristo Mountains (see Day 4's Travel Route),
opted to invest its government funding in Santa Fe tourism. The hotel provides employment and the main
source of income for the pueblo. Its location is about
eight blocks walk from the plaza, and a free shuttle runs
between the hotel and downtown every half hour. Rates
start at $110 during the summer season.

Other luxury hotels within walking distance of the
plaza include **La Fonda**, 100 E. San Francisco, (505)
982-5511, Santa Fe's oldest hotel and still one of the best
($125 double); and **Hotel St. Francis**, 210 Don Gaspar,

(505) 983-5700, newly renovated as an elegant small
hotel ($90-$150 double). The newest downtown hotels,
both in renovated historic buildings a block from the
plaza, are two small, ultrachic European-style lodgings.
The **Hotel Plaza Real**, 125 Washington Avenue, (505)
988-4900, has a peaceful inner courtyard and 56 guest
rooms and suites decorated in elegantly rustic Southwestern style. Most rooms have wood-burning fireplaces
and patios or balconies. Rates run $115 to $145 (about
20% lower off-season), with suites up to $425 a night.
Next door, the **Inn of the Anasazi**, 113 Washington Avenue, (505) 988-3030 or (800) 988-3030, overflows with
Santa Fe style, its 59 guest rooms and suites, which blend
traditional and modern furnishings, feature gaslit fireplaces and special little touches like organic cedar-scented
toiletries and handwoven rugs and fabrics. Room rates
run $190 to $240 (about 15% lower off-season) with
suites to $395 a night.

Santa Fe has several bed-and-breakfast inns. Since a
city ordinance restricts B&Bs to areas with commercial
zoning, most are within easy walking distance of the
plaza. My favorite, because its small size (just five guest
rooms—with feather mattresses) makes for an exceptionally homelike atmosphere, is the **Inn of the Animal
Tracks**, 707 Paseo de Peralta, (505) 988-1546. Innkeeper
Daun Martin formerly managed the famous Britt House in
San Diego and is as close to a perfect hostess as you'll ever
meet. Her love for animals pervades the house (each
guest bedroom has a different animal theme), but since
she keeps pets on the premises, guests cannot bring
theirs. The $85 to $110 room rates include a full breakfast
as well as afternoon tea and dessert—the best homemade
pies in town. For more formal bed-and-breakfast accommodations, go to the **Grant Corner Inn**, 122 Grant,
(505) 983-6678, a turn-of-the-century brick mansion
across from the Furr's supermarket a block west and a
block north of the Fine Arts Museum, where rates range
from $60 to $135 double, full breakfast included.

A new, small, very upscale bed and breakfast is **Dos**

Casas Viejas, 610 Agua Fria Street, (505) 983-1636. Located in an economically-mixed, historic residential neighborhood about a mile west of the Plaza, this quiet, secluded compound with high walls and an electronic security gate offers privacy and peace, along with a 40-foot swimming pool, a library with fireplace, and poolside dining. There are only three units—a standard room at $125, a minisuite at $175, and a two-room suite at $185. All have kiva fireplaces, ceiling fans, large patios, and private entrances. Approximately a dozen other Santa Fe bed and breakfasts can be booked through Santa Fe Central Reservations, (505) 983-8200 or (800) 982-7669 outside of New Mexico.

You'll find several lower-cost motels along busy Cerrillos Road, which runs for miles diagonally southwest from downtown. The best rates close to downtown are at the **Santa Fe Travelodge**, 646 Cerrillos Road, (505) 982-3551, where doubles start at $48.

Warning: Santa Fe accommodations tend to fill up quickly on Wednesday through Saturday nights during Opera season, mid-July through mid-August, so if you are traveling without reservations, check into your hotel or motel as soon as you arrive in town, before sightseeing or eating. Another warning: for Indian Market weekend, the third weekend in August, all accommodations in the Santa Fe area are booked up as much as four months in advance, and it may be impossible to find lodging on short notice even in Albuquerque or Los Alamos!

Food

Green chile is what distinguishes New Mexican cuisine from any other. New Mexicans grow more chile peppers than the rest of the United States combined and prefer to eat them as a roasted, peeled, and usually diced vegetable, by the bowlful or poured over practically anything. The quality of chile is judged by how "hot" it is, so restaurants compete to bring tears of ecstasy to their patrons' eyes. When a waitress asks, "Red or green?" don't make the common error of assuming that green must be milder than red. The green chile at any self-respecting Santa Fe restaurant will knock your socks off.

For regional cuisine in Santa Fe, there are myriad possibilities. **Tomasita's**, 500 S. Guadalupe, (505) 983-5721, has good New Mexican lunches and dinners, including daily specials, at moderate prices. **The Burrito Company**, just off the plaza on Washington Street, serves Mexican fast food smothered in green chile and has a sidewalk patio perfect for people-watching. **Tia Sophia's**, 210 W. San Francisco, is an unpretentious coffee shop for breakfast or lunch. The spicy food here is guaranteed to wake you up!

Santa Fe has about 200 restaurants, constantly changing, serving everything from Greek grape leaves to green chile tempura. Pick up a current restaurant guide from the La Fonda tourist information desk for an array of possibilities. When stocking up on picnic supplies, be sure to pick up a loaf or two of the delicious homemade bread, baked in horno ovens, that Indian vendors sell on the streets around the plaza. The only way to take green chile back home is in the form of jelly, jam, or relish, available in many gift shops. Other great edible souvenirs are piñon nuts, red chile ristras, and Indian blue corn. Blue corn tortilla chips are sold in Santa Fe supermarkets. Blue cornmeal can be boiled into a tasty hot cereal called atole, similar to cream of wheat, or substituted in any recipe that uses cornmeal (use buttermilk instead of regular milk for a brighter blue color). Pueblo Indians, who hold blue corn sacred, make it into a crisp paper-thin bread called piki for festivals and religious ceremonies.

Nightlife

From the moment you leave Santa Fe until you reach Las Vegas two weeks from now, evening entertainment will consist of crackling campfires, spectacularly starry skies, and an occasional ranger slide show. If you want to get out and boogie, tonight's the night.

The larger downtown hotels all have lounges, piano bars, or the like. For quiet, cozy elegance, stop in at the

Staab House bar in La Posada, east of Paseo de Peralta on Palace Avenue, with its authentic Victorian era furnishings and notorious resident ghost. Ask anyone who works there about her.

Chez What?, 213 W. Alameda, 982-0099, at the southwest edge of downtown, lures a widely mixed audience with an eclectic assortment of high-energy live music. Tonight it might be rock 'n roll, African pop, Texas blues, or salsa music; or it could be the only chance you'll ever have to see Indians dance to a reggae beat. Cover charge varies; music starts at 9:30 p.m. nightly. A good place to meet Santa Fe locals is **El Farol** on Canyon Road at Palace Avenue, a friendly neighborhood bar in an uncommon neighborhood. Folk musicians perform some nights for a small cover. There are rarely any open tables after 9:00 p.m. Join a group of strangers and you'll find yourself welcome. It's that kind of place.

Santa Fe's summer calendar is packed with cultural performances and spectator events. The most famous is the **Santa Fe Opera**, on US 285 3 miles north of town, mid-July through mid-August. Tickets are expensive and hard to get on short notice, but if you dress as elegantly as possible (wearing blue jeans to the opera is considered déclassé, though many locals used to and some still do) and ask at the box office, your chances of getting inexpensive standing-room tickets and finding vacant seats later are good. Call 982-3855 for information.

For something completely different in the way of theater entertainment, consider the **Madrid Melodrama**, held during the summer months in the town of Madrid, which you went through on the Turquoise Trail this morning. Melodramas for tourists can be found throughout the west in the summer, but this one is the most authentic I've ever witnessed, with its straight-faced presentations of genuine Victorian plays in an old railroad barn that recalls the kinds of places where touring companies actually performed in small towns a century ago. The playhouse even has a real locomotive, adding realism when the script calls for a heroine to be tied to the railroad tracks. Bring a bag of marshmallows and learn first-hand why they came to be known as "villain bullets." Tickets cost $6.50. Call 473-0743 for current performance information.

Other events range from the **Santa Fe Chamber Music Festival** to the **Rodeo de Santa Fe**. Check the weekly (Thursday to Wednesday) *Reporter* or the *New Mexican*'s Friday "Pasatiempo" supplement for complete entertainment listings and reviews.

Itinerary Option: Pecos

For a pleasant afternoon outdoors, drive about 20 miles east (northbound) from Santa Fe on I-25 to the second Pecos exit and visit Pecos National Historical Park, the site of a major pueblo ruin that dates back to the thirteenth century A.D. and a Spanish mission from the seventeenth century. The Pecos pueblo was the eastern gateway to the Rio Grande pueblo country, and it prospered through trade. A long, massive wall, still partly standing, separated the pueblo from the camping area for visiting groups of Indians from the eastern plains. The pueblo was abandoned in the mid-1800s after Comanche raids wiped out much of the population, and the survivors' descendants now live at Jemez Pueblo in the mountains north of Albuquerque. Open daily from 8:00 a.m. to 5:00 p.m. during the summer months, until 5:00 p.m. the rest of the year. Admission is $1 per person, maximum $3 per carload.

Until last year, the park was a national monument, just 365 acres in size. In response to citizen concerns about development in the area, the U.S. government authorized acquisition of the adjoining 5,500-acre ranch owned by actress Greer Garson. It also added two tracts of land nearby where the westernmost battle of the Civil War took place and changed the monument to a national historical park. I, and many others, can hardly wait for the park service to open the newly acquired ranchlands to the public, since they include a beautiful 2-mile stretch of the Pecos River well removed from the highway. But the planning process is scheduled to take three years, and the new land probably won't be open to hikers before 1995.

After visiting the park, you may wish to continue west through the village and enjoy a scenic 20-mile drive up the Pecos River Canyon, a popular trout fishing area with enclaves of vacation cabins. The pavement ends at the Terrero General Store, and from there an unpaved road that can be quite rough and hard on vehicles leads to a series of free campgrounds and trailheads at the edge of the Pecos Wilderness. Midway up the paved portion of the road, a dirt road turns off into Dalton Canyon, used as a hideout by the notorious outlaw Dalton Gang for many years in the late nineteenth century. The canyon is a pretty spot for walking and picnicking.

BANDELIER NATIONAL MONUMENT AND LOS ALAMOS

Los Alamos, White Rock, and Bandelier National Monument occupy parts of the Pajarito Plateau, a ledge of lava and ash formed by a huge volcano. If you could view the area from above, you would see that the mountain range to the west is actually circular, the crumbled remains of the rim of the volcano, which some geologists believe stood higher than Mount Everest some 1,700,000 years ago. The entire area has been nominated for national park status three times—first in 1919 and most recently in 1986. While all three attempts have been blocked by the forest products industry, nobody has ever doubted that the area's scenic beauty and unique features rival those of the Grand Canyon, Yosemite, or Yellowstone. Here, side by side, you'll find pre-Columbian Indian ruins and the birthplace of the nuclear age.

The area is a one-hour drive from Santa Fe. Along the way you can visit an outdoor sculpture gallery and a modern Indian pueblo.

Suggested Schedule

8:00 a.m.	Breakfast.
9:00 a.m.	Drive to Bandelier National Monument, visiting Shidoni's sculpture gardens and San Ildefonso Pueblo en route.
11:00 a.m.	Arrive at Bandelier. Explore the Indian ruins and enjoy a picnic lunch.
2:00 p.m.	Stay in Bandelier for an afternoon of hiking or explore the Los Alamos area.
5:00 p.m.	Take your choice: return to Santa Fe, camp in Bandelier, or spend the night in Los Alamos or White Rock.

Travel Route: Santa Fe to Bandelier National Monument (40 miles)

Leave Santa Fe on Bishop's Lodge Road and drive 5 miles to Tesuque, stopping at Shidoni Art Foundry (watch for it

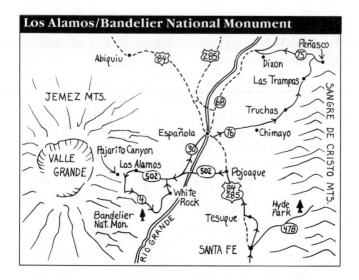

Los Alamos/Bandelier National Monument

on your left) to walk around acres of parklike outdoor sculpture gallery. If you own a skyscraper or shopping mall and want a really large piece of art to put in front of it, here's where you can buy one.

Join US 285 northbound at Tesuque for 9 miles to the Los Alamos-Bandelier exit on the left, and follow NM 502 west.

After about 5 miles, you'll see the turnoff on the right to San Ildefonso Pueblo. In another 3 miles, you'll cross the Rio Grande. (Bandelier, your destination, is just 17 miles from Santa Fe as the crow flies, but you have to drive more than twice that distance because this is the only bridge over the river.) The road divides 4 miles past the river, one fork going to Los Alamos and the other to White Rock and Bandelier.

Leaving Bandelier, if you turn left from the entrance instead of backtracking to the right, you will reach a shortcut to Los Alamos in a few miles. This road takes you past Pajarito Canyon, one of the Pajarito Plateau sightseeing highlights mentioned below. When you pass the Los Alamos National Laboratories administration buildings, where the Bradbury Science Museum is located, turn left at the stoplight, cross the bridge, and then turn right on Trinity Drive to reach the Los Alamos central business district. Jog one block north at the first opportunity to reach the historical museum and Fuller Lodge Art Gallery.

Leaving Los Alamos, Trinity Drive will put you back on NM 502 for a spectacular descent along the canyon wall.

Sightseeing Highlights

▲ **San Ildefonso Pueblo**—While the most striking Indian pueblos in New Mexico, Taos (Day 4) and Ácoma (Day 22), seem like fragments of the past, San Ildefonso typifies modern-day pueblos along the Rio Grande. The central plaza is much larger than those at most other pueblos; San Ildefonso has two separate kiva clans, so during ceremonies two dances are often held simultaneously on opposite sides of the plaza. The mission-style church was built around 1970 to replace an old one. Behind the pueblo rises a massive volcanic rock formation called Black Mesa. A sacred spot to the San Ildefonso people, whose ancestors retreated to live on top of it when the Spanish returned after the Pueblo Revolt of 1680, the mesa is forbidden to non-Indians.

The distinctive rakulike black pottery style developed at San Ildefonso by the late Maria Martinez (a film about her is shown at national parks and monuments throughout the Four Corners area) is prized by collectors and found in museums around the world. A collection of Maria's pottery can be seen upon request at the Popovi Da Studio in the pueblo, open daily during the summer months from 10:00 a.m. to 5:00 p.m., closed weekends and Wednesdays during May and October. Arts and crafts are more important than ever to this pueblo. The pueblo has a small museum, open during the summer on weekdays only from 8:00 a.m. to 5:00 p.m.

▲▲▲ **Bandelier National Monument**—The birthplace of southwestern archaeology, now a hikers' paradise, is named for Adolph Bandelier, a Swiss immigrant and self-taught Native American scholar. In 1880, he was the first southwestern archaeologist to excavate and study Indian ruins instead of looting them for collectible artifacts. Unexcavated pueblo ruins, found throughout the Jemez Mountains, are crumbled, buried, hard to recognize, not much to look at. Bandelier's excavation was the prototype for restoring all the Anasazi ruins that are visitor attractions today.

The ruins behind the visitors center stand as the crowning achievement of Bandelier's thirty-four years of work. The settlement dates from the postclassical Pueblo period (A.D. 1400, after the decline of the Chaco culture, of which you'll see more in a few days).

Only a stone floor plan remains of what was once a three-story castlelike walled town, while nearby cliff dwellings are better preserved. Climb to the Ceremonial Cave for the best view of the ruins and their magnificent canyon setting.

The road takes you in only to the corner of the monument; beyond the visitors center and ruins is a large, rugged hikers-only wilderness area. A round-trip hike to the far boundary would take three full days. For an enjoyable day hike, explore more of Frijoles Canyon. The Falls Trail, downstream from the end of the backpackers' parking area across the bridge from the visitors center, is a 1½-mile (one-way) hike that packs cool creekside forests, cliffs, volcanic tent rocks, and a lovely waterfall view into a challenging 2½-hour hike. For a longer, all-afternoon or even all-day excursion, get a free wilderness permit from the visitors center and hike the Upper Frijoles Trail, rock-hopping and sometimes splashing back and forth across the creek. Watch for golden eagles, turkey vultures, and red-tailed hawks overhead. Go as far as you like; the trail continues about 8 miles to the upper end of Frijoles Canyon. (This is a more enjoyable day hike than the more popular Stone Lions Trail, a hot trip that's much more strenuous than it appears on the map because midway it traverses Alamo Canyon, both deeper and steeper than Frijoles Canyon.)

Admission to the national monument is $5 per vehicle. Instead, you may want to buy a Golden Eagle Pass, good for free admission to all national parks and monuments for the rest of the calendar year. The cash savings from using the pass on this trip will be significant. It will encourage you to visit less-known U.S. fee areas you might otherwise skip, and flashing your pass at the entrance will make you feel like a VIP.

▲▲ **Los Alamos**—The hidden site of the ultimate Top Secret Government Project during World War II is now a cozy all-American community with incomparable views. People here work at the nuclear research laboratory, so big you can't miss it. (You can't go in, either.) To learn more about high technology and/or the birth of the bomb, visit the outstanding Bradbury Science Museum, where you'll see mementos of the Manhattan Project, hands-on computer and laser exhibits, an antique atomic bomb, and explanations of other technologies developed at the labs which are difficult to pronounce, let alone comprehend. Open Tuesday through Friday from 9:00 a.m. to 5:00 p.m., Saturday through Monday 1:00 to 5:00 p.m., the museum is located next to the LANL administration building near the stoplight across the Los Alamos Canyon bridge from downtown. Admission is free.

The Los Alamos County Historical Museum and Fuller Lodge Art Center occupy buildings of the pre-World War II Los Alamos Ranch School, where children from wealthy eastern families were sent to get healthy through outdoor living. The historical museum tells about the joys and rigors of life at the ranch school, as well as the war years at Los Alamos. Fuller Lodge Art Center provides exhibition space for a community cooperative of local artists, a refreshing contrast to Santa Fe's big-money art market. Near the corner of Central Avenue and 20th Street, both museums are open Monday through Saturday from 10:00 a.m. to 4:00 p.m., Sunday 1:00 to 4:00 p.m. There is a small pueblo ruin in the park behind the lodge.

▲ **Pajarito Plateau and Valle Grande**—If Congress were to create Pajarito National Park or Jemez National Park (the names that have actually been proposed), the following little-known spots would be a few of the points of interest:

White Rock Overlook—As you drive into the Los Alamos bedroom community of White Rock on your way to Bandelier National Monument, turn left on Rover Drive and follow the signs to White Rock Overlook in a municipal park on the tip of the mesa. Seven hundred feet below runs a seemingly untouched wild stretch of the Rio Grande. To the north, Black Mesa looms at the end of the canyon, and beyond it you can see the rugged Sangre de Cristo Mountains running all the way up into Colorado. Behind you, a thin waterfall plunges into a side canyon. The only way to reach the river below is by a steep trail that descends to the canyon bottom in less than a mile. You can see the trail toward your right from the overlook, but finding its starting point is trickier. The trailhead, well hidden near the picnic ground about a hundred yards to the right of the overlook, is marked only by two old fence posts on the rim.

Pajarito Canyon—Follow NM 501, the paved road that goes west (uphill, toward the mountains) from the stoplight near the LANL administration building and the science museum. The road curves around to the south and passes a paved side road on the right that goes to the Los Alamos ski area. Continue on NM 503 for about half a mile and watch for the next road on the right, an un-paved, unmarked forest road that runs in both directions parallel to the main road. Park beside this road and follow the dirt road north (downhill); it curves to the west, fol-lowing a small creek, and ends after a quarter of a mile, but a trail continues up Pajarito Canyon from here. What distinguishes this from all the other dozen or so canyons in the area is the narrow passageway between the rock walls which prevented timber from being cut in the can-yon. This is the only untouched old growth forest in the Jemez Mountains, lush and magnificent. Locals refer to it as "the rain forest." Black bears are sometimes spotted farther back in the canyon.

Valle Grande—Continuing on NM 503 west for about 10 steep miles beyond the entrance to Bandelier National Monument, you will reach the upper rim of the Jemez Mountains and soon see Valle Grande, which is said to be the world's largest volcano caldera, with a smaller, more recent volcano cone in its center. It would look very much like Crater Lake in Oregon, except that a narrow canyon on the far side lets the water run out. Is the volcano extinct? Consider the fact that dozens of hot springs exist throughout the area. On the west side of the caldera, Los Alamos National Laboratories maintains a geothermal pilot project to experiment with ways to convert the earth's heat to useful energy. Something is causing all that heat so close beneath the surface. Extinct? Don't bet on it.

Cliff Dwellings—There are over ten thousand known archaeological sites on the Pajarito Plateau. If you look closely, you can see the remnants of cliff dwellings on the south-facing side of every canyon, most easily spotted by the man-made holes that once held roof supports. In fact, around A.D. 1400, more people lived in this area than are here today. If you watch along the sides of any highway in the Los Alamos area, you will see locked gates that often have two white signs lettered too small to read and a walkway at the side of the gate. The signs do not say "Keep out." One says that camping, hunting, and certain other activities are prohibited; the other warns that it is against the law to remove Indian artifacts—a good indication that Indian ruins are there. As long as the area is not posted with "No trespassing" signs, you are free to enter and explore. (If there are "No trespassing" signs, heed them absolutely. Remember that back in the 1940s they were very casual about disposing of nuclear waste, and a few areas around Los Alamos are permanently radioactive!)

Camping

Bandelier's mesa-top campground has an easy trail to the canyon rim for evening walks as well as nightly campfire

talks and running water. Camping costs $7 plus admission
to the national monument. There are no hookups.

There is a free municipal campground with dumping
station one mile east of Los Alamos, beside the highway
just before the beginning of the canyon descent.

Lodging

The nearest motel to Bandelier is the **White Rock Motor
Lodge**, (505) 672-3838, 10 miles northeast of the monument entrance on NM Loop 4 in the town of White Rock.
Some rooms have kitchenettes, and all have satellite TV.
Rooms cost $50 per night double. Los Alamos has two
motels—the **Hilltop House** at Trinity and Central, (505)
662-2441, with rooms starting at $64 per night, and the
Los Alamos Inn, 2201 Trinity, (505) 662-7211, with
rooms starting at $63 double.

Food

In Bandelier National Monument, a small snack bar
adjoins the gift shop near the visitors center.

White Rock has five restaurants, all moderately priced.
Try **Cheers Family Restaurant**, 672-3661, for soup,
sandwiches, Mexican food, and breakfast served all day,
open Monday 9:30 a.m. to 8:00 p.m., Tuesday through
Saturday 6:30 a.m. to 9:00 p.m., and Sunday 7:00 a.m. to
3:00 p.m. In Los Alamos, **Colores Restaurant** at 820
Trinity, 662-6285, serves New Mexican food for lunch
(weekdays only) from 11:00 a.m. to 3:00 p.m. and dinner
from 5:00 to 8:00 p.m. **Boccaccio's**, on the golf course
at 4244 Diamond Drive, 662-7204, features steaks, seafood, and pasta for lunch (weekdays only) from 11:30
a.m. to 2:00 p.m. and dinner (Tuesday through Saturday)
from 5:30 to 8:30 p.m., Friday until 9:00 p.m.

TAOS AND THE GREAT SAND DUNES

This will be the first full driving day of your trip, with an intermission in Taos. The High Road to Taos takes you through old Spanish colonial villages and into Carson National Forest, then descends to Rio Grande State Park. In the Taos area, visit Taos Pueblo and perhaps D. H. Lawrence's ranch. Later in the afternoon, drive north to Great Sand Dunes National Monument. Hike the dunes.

Suggested Schedule

8:30 a.m.	Break camp. Drive to Española, Chimayo, and the High Road to Taos, stopping at Picurís Pueblo and then descending through Dixon.
11:00 a.m.	Drive through Rio Grande State Park to Taos.
12:00 noon	Lunch, see Taos.
1:30 p.m.	Visit Taos Pueblo.
2:30 p.m.	Stop at D. H. Lawrence Ranch or Millicent Rogers Museum.
3:30 p.m.	Drive to Great Sand Dunes.
5:30 p.m.	Camp at Great Sand Dunes or take a motel in Alamosa.

Travel Route: Los Alamos to Taos (99 miles)

From Los Alamos, White Rock, or Bandelier, descend the Pajarito Plateau on NM 502 and, before reaching the Rio Grande, turn left on the paved back road to Española, which parallels the river and takes you past Black Mesa and Santa Clara Pueblo. The road to Puye Cliff Dwellings turns off to the west midway along this road. The cliff dwellings, the ancestral home of the Santa Clara people since the twelfth century A.D., extend in several levels for about 2 miles along the face of the cliff. You can see the cliff dwellings at a distance before deciding whether to pay the $4 per person admission charge, which goes to Santa Clara Pueblo. There is also a large pueblo ruin on

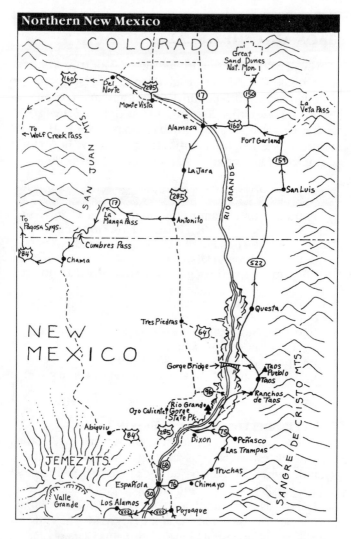

Northern New Mexico

top of the mesa, partially restored and still used for ceremonies by residents of the modern pueblo.

From Española, turn right and drive through town to
find NM 76 east to Chimayo, 10 miles into the foothills of
the Sangre de Cristo range. As you approach Chimayo,
watch for the sign to "Santuario" and follow it. Santuario

de Chimayo, a small twin-towered church built entirely without nails in 1816, is believed by northern New Mexico's Catholics to be a place of miracles—the Lourdes of the American frontier. In a small room through another room to the left of the altar is El Pozito ("the little well"), where for over two centuries the faithful have taken pinches of clay for its healing properties. The crutches and braces in the adjoining room have been left as testimony that it works. Between Good Friday and Easter, thousands of people from throughout northern New Mexico line the roads, some carrying crosses, in pilgrimage to Chimayo.

Return to NM 76 and continue north up and down the hills. This is the most picturesque segment of the High Road to Taos. Each valley has a small village of farmers and woodcutters which dates back to Spanish colonial times. At the base of 13,102-foot Truchas Peak, Truchas (the name means "trout") was used in 1986 as the filming location for *The Milagro Beanfield War*, directed by Robert Redford from New Mexico author John Nichols's novel. Just off the highway at Las Trampas ("the traps") is an imposing mission church that dates back to 1751.

At Picurís (San Lorenzo) Pueblo, near the village of Peñasco, NM 76 ends in a T-intersection with NM 75. Secluded in its mountain valley, Picurís Pueblo has a restaurant, a fishing lake, and a small museum, where you can see examples of the unusual micaceous pottery that has been made here for 800 years. Mica in the local clay gives the pots an iridescent, almost bronzelike appearance. This pottery has recently become popular among Indian pottery collectors. While most residents of Picurís Pueblo live in government project housing, the ancient pueblo is being restored, and tours are available for a small fee.

From the highway intersection at Picurís, following the signs to Taos—turning right and then, 7 miles later, left on NM 518 through Carson National Forest—is the shorter (26 miles) but not much faster route. I suggest, instead, that you turn left (west) on NM 75, which will take you down a continuous 17-mile descent to the Rio

Grande, passing through the artists-and-apple-orchards
community of Dixon. When you return to NM 68, turn
right (north) and go 10 miles to Pilar. Turn left, following
the sign to Orillo Verde Recreation Area (formerly Rio
Grande State Park). A $2 day-use fee is charged for pic-
nicking in the park but not for driving through. The road
follows the riverbank up the gorge, past several picnic
areas. When the pavement ends, turn right (east). The
road climbs out of the canyon, affording a good view of
the Taos Valley with Wheeler Peak (at 13,161 feet, the
highest mountain in New Mexico) in the background.
Soon the pavement resumes and zips you back to the
main highway just south of Ranchos de Taos.

Taos
The northernmost outpost of Spanish colonial America,
founded five years after Santa Fe, Taos was the third permanent European settlement in what's now the United
States. It was a major center for trade with people who
weren't allowed farther into Spanish territory—the
Navajo, Ute, and plains tribes as well as French and Anglo
mountain men.

In 1898, two American artists, Bert Phillips and Ernest
Blumenschein, were bound for Mexico on a sketching
expedition but made it only as far as Taos before their
wagon broke down. Enchanted by the land, the exotic
people, and the strangely vivid quality of the light, they
stayed to form the nucleus of Taos' active artist community. Other artists came to Taos from Europe at the out-
break of World War I, and beginning in the 1920s, the
town's cultural scene enjoyed international renown as the
"Left Bank" of the American frontier.

Taos depends almost entirely on tourism and the arts
(perhaps a natural continuation of the town's historic
role—trading with "barbarians" from the north). With its
beautiful natural setting and rich tricultural heritage, it
may be among the best places in the world to live if you
don't need a job. The largest employer in Taos County is
the Highway Department.

Entering Taos along three congested miles of strip city, you'll go up a block-long hill as you enter the historic district. Turn left at the top of the hill to the pretty, modernized town plaza.

Taos Sightseeing Highlights

▲ **Kit Carson Home and Museum**—On Kit Carson Road (Highway 64) just across the main highway from the plaza area, this 12-room adobe was Kit Carson's home for 25 years from 1843 to 1868. It houses a museum of territorial period antiques and a small chapel. Open daily from 8:00 a.m. to 6:00 p.m. during the summer months, 9:00 a.m. to 5:00 p.m. the rest of the year; admission $3 for adults, $2.50 for senior citizens, $2 for children ages 6 to 15, maximum $6 per family. Kit Carson's grave is two blocks to the north in the park named after him.

▲ **Blumenschein Home**—On Ledoux Street one block south of the plaza, this 1797 adobe house was the home and studio of Ernest Blumenschein, a founder in 1915 of the Taos Society of Artists. Changing art exhibits, European antiques, and handmade Taos furniture are on display. Open daily from 9:00 a.m. to 5:00 p.m.; admission $3 for adults, $2.50 for senior citizens, $2 for children ages 6 to 15, maximum $6 per family.

▲▲ **Martinez Hacienda**—This is the only remaining Spanish colonial hacienda in New Mexico open to the public on a regular basis. Built in 1804 as a fortresslike refuge from Comanche raids, it has thick adobe walls and no exterior windows. To find it, follow Ranchitos Road west from the plaza until you reach the Rio Grande. The 21-room hacienda is on the riverbank. Open daily from 9:00 a.m. to 5:00 p.m.; admission $3 for adults, $2.50 for senior citizens, $2 for children ages 6 to 15, maximum $6 per family.

▲▲▲ **Taos Pueblo**—The oldest and best-known of the Rio Grande Indian pueblos, now a National Historic Landmark, preserves the multistory architectural style that dates back to the twelfth century. About 1,400 people live in the pueblo today. Ceremonies and dances held at the pueblo include the Fiesta of San Antonio on June 13, a corn dance in late June, a three-day powwow in early July, and the Fiesta of San Geronimo on the evening of September 29 and all day September 30. Call the pueblo at (505) 758-8626 for more information. To reach the pueblo, continue north from the plaza on NM 68 for about 2 miles and watch for the turnoff on your right. Open to the public daily from 8:00 a.m. to 6:00 p.m. during the summer months, 9:00 a.m. to 4:30 p.m. the rest of the year. A $5 parking fee is charged, and photography fees are $5 for still cameras and $10 for movie or video cameras; no cameras are allowed during ceremonies.

▲ **Millicent Rogers Museum**—Founded in 1953 and relocated to its present building in 1968, this museum houses one of the most extensive private collections of Indian art in the Southwest. Featured are Navajo and Pueblo jewelry, Navajo textiles, Pueblo pottery and paintings, Hopi and Zuñi kachinas, and basketry from several Native American cultures as well as some Spanish colonial folk art items. To get there, go 4 miles north of Taos on the main highway; turn left just before the blinking light and follow the signs. Open daily from 9:00 a.m. to 5:00 p.m.; admission $3 for adults, $2 for students and senior citizens, $1 for children ages 6 to 16, maximum $6 per family.

▲ **D. H. Lawrence Ranch**—The British novelist, whose books stirred controversy on both sides of the Atlantic, took refuge here during 1924-25 to escape public notoriety. His widow, Frieda, willed the ranch to the University of New Mexico on condition that ten acres of the property, including the ranch buildings and shrine, always remain open to the public. While Lawrence never wrote a major work with a New Mexico setting, writers and readers from all over the world visit to draw inspiration from the Lawrence Shrine. Lawrence's ashes may be blended into the concrete slab in the shrine. (Somebody's are, anyway. So the story goes, there was a mix-up of urns at U.S. Customs in New York when the ashes were being brought from France. An appropriate postscript to an enigmatic life.) To reach the ranch, take the marked turn-off on the left, about 7 miles north of Taos on NM 68. The shrine is 100 yards uphill from the visitor parking area.

Besides writing, Lawrence once tried his hand at the visual arts. Amateurish though his attempts may have been, his paintings scandalized London and resulted in an obscenity prosecution that drove him from England for the last time. You can view the naughty pictures and judge for yourself for $3 in a back room of La Fonda de Taos on the town plaza.

▲ **Rio Grande Gorge Bridge**—The only bridge across the gorge, affording a spectacular view of this stretch of the Rio Grande protected under the federal Wild and Scenic Rivers Act, is on US 64 (the highway to Tres Piedras), about 10 miles west of the intersection with NM 68, which is 4 miles north of Taos.

▲ **Wild Rivers Recreation Area**—This new recreation area at the confluence of the Rio Grande and Red River 20 miles from Taos—turn left 3 miles north of Questa on NM 378 and follow the signs—has been the launching area for raft trips through the Taos Box on the Rio Grande for many years. It became so heavily used that in 1990, the federal government declared its new, official status and built a visitor center. Other amenities include hiking trails, hot springs by the river's edge, and campsites on the canyon rim. Camping costs $6; admission to the recreation area is free.

Travel Route: Taos to Great Sand Dunes National Monument (130 miles)

From Taos, continue north on NM 522 (which becomes CO 159 as it crosses the state line) for 79 miles, following the Sangre de Cristo Mountains along the eastern side of the San Luis Valley through San Luis, Colorado's oldest town, founded in 1851. The small museum and cultural center in San Luis contains an excellent exhibit, funded by the National Endowment for the Humanities, explaining the history of the valley and its people. CO 159 joins US 160 near Fort Garland, an 1850s U.S. Army outpost

once commanded by Kit Carson and now a Colorado
State Historic Site. This route is known as the Kit Carson
Highway.

Though just up the river from Taos, the San Luis Valley
wasn't explored by the Spanish for nearly two centuries.
In 1779, the conquistador De Anza braved hostile
Comanche bands to make it up as far as Alamosa, where
the Rio Grande veers west to its headwaters in the San
Juan Mountains. The discovery astonished mapmakers of
the time, who had always assumed that the river came
from the North Pole. U.S. Army occupation in the mid-
1800s made the valley safe for Hispanic settlers, whose
descendants live there today.

From Fort Garland, turn left (west) on US 160 and go 10
miles to the turnoff on the right (north) to Great Sand
Dunes National Monument. From there, it's 16 miles to
the monument entrance gate.

Great Sand Dunes National Monument
Like a beach in reverse, a wide shallow ribbon of cold
mountain stream water lies along the edge of a vast and
awesome expanse of sand. Beyond the picnic area turnoff
near the visitors center, a mostly local crowd basks on
beach towels beside beer coolers while the kids con-
struct sand castles along the creek. It could be time to
break out the bathing suits, even though the water is only
two inches deep.

The sand dunes, the largest in the United States, formed
as millennia of sandstorms swept the San Luis Valley, as
they still do, dropping their loads of sand in a pile where
the wind funnels into the mountains. The dunes are 900
feet high and cover an area of 60 square miles. To get a
sense of how big the dunes really are, take out your
binoculars and watch tiny hikers struggle toward the sum-
mits. For an even better sense, climb one yourself (allow
two hours up, half an hour back) and, when you finally
reach the top, you'll be rewarded by a view of many more
miles of sand. A less crowded dune area is reached by a
trail that leads from the campground past where escape

dunes have engulfed the ponderosa forest.

Often used as an "alien planet" location for science fiction movies, the dunes also offer incomparable photographic opportunities. Particularly in early morning and late afternoon as shadows deepen, their weird abstractions challenge the eye. No two photographers' pictures of the sand dunes look alike. When hiking on the sand, wrap your camera in a plastic bag to protect the lens and mechanism from grit.

Entrance to the monument is $5 unless you have a Golden Eagle or Golden Age pass. Open year-round.

Camping
The 88-site **Piñon Flats Campground** at Great Sand Dunes National Monument has tables, fire grills, convenient rest rooms, and nightly campfire talks. All campsites have fine views of the dunes. Deer are abundant and may bound right through your camp. The campground area also teems with chipmunks, ground squirrels, and cottontail rabbits. Both the dunes trail and the Medano Pass Primitive Road that intersects it are ideal for sunset walking. The camping fee is $5. There are no hookups.

Full hookups are available at the **Great Sand Dunes Oasis** outside the park for $12.50. They also offer horseback riding and four-wheel-drive tours into the backcountry dunes.

Within the park, backcountry camping is allowed (free permit required, campfires prohibited) at **Sand Pit** and **Castle Creek**, 1½ and 2 miles up Medano Creek Primitive Road. Unless you have four-wheel drive, don't even think of driving on this road—the minimum tow charge for getting unstuck from the sand is $100. If you're fully equipped for backpacking, there is a hikers-only campground a quarter-mile from the road at mile 4.

Lodging
Alamosa, 32 miles from Great Sand Dunes, is your best bet for motel accommodations. The **Best Western Alamosa Inn**, 1919 Main Street, (719) 589-2567, has an

indoor pool; doubles start at $69 in summer, $57 off-season. The **Holiday Inn**, 333 Santa Fe Avenue, (719) 589-5833, also has an indoor pool as well as a sauna and whirlpool. Rates start at $69. Lower-priced lodging can be found at the **American Inn**, 2505 Main Street, (719) 589-6447, where doubles start around $40. All three motels have cable color television.

A gentleman from Washington, D.C., who used the first edition of this book enthusiastically recommends the new **Cottonwood Inn** at 123 San Juan Avenue in Alamosa. Although his suggestion came too late for me to check it out, he calls it "one of the nicest and best-run bed and breakfasts that we stayed in anywhere." For rates and reservations, call (719) 589-3882.

Food

I hope you brought some. Otherwise, a limited selection of groceries and microwave sandwiches is available at the **Great Sand Dunes Oasis** store. The nearest restaurant to Great Sand Dunes is the unpretentious little roadside café at Fort Garland.

OVER THE MOUNTAINS TO MESA VERDE

Since you left Albuquerque, you've followed the Rio
Grande north for over 250 miles. Today you'll head west
across the Great Divide to the Four Corners region, so
called because the conjunction of Colorado, New Mexico, Arizona, and Utah—marked by a small monument
(which isn't worth going out of your way for) beside US
160 an hour's drive southwest of Mesa Verde—is the only
place in the United States where four states meet.
Durango is the region's major town and tourism center.
You'll spend most of today driving there.

Suggested Schedule

8:00 a.m.	Hike the dunes.
10:30 a.m.	Drive to Antonito.
12:30 p.m.	Drive to Chama, Cumbres Pass picnic.
2:30 p.m.	Drive to Durango.
5:00 p.m.	Drive to Mesa Verde and camp, or spend the night in Durango.

Travel Route: Sand Dunes to Mesa Verde—Direct (238 miles) or Scenic (304 miles)

Leaving Great Sand Dunes National Monument by the
same 16-mile road you came in on, turn right (west) on
US 160 and drive 16 more miles into Alamosa (pop.
7,000), the largest town in the San Luis Valley. There, at
the junction of US 160 and US 285, you face a choice.

Durango lies on the other side of the Continental
Divide, at the southwestern edge of the San Juan Mountains, the massive range you see to the west. The well-
trodden tourist trail from Alamosa to Durango follows US
160 the whole way, about a 4-hour drive. The main scenic attraction on the route, and at the same time the
major drawback, is 10,850-foot Wolf Creek Pass. Legend-
ary among truck drivers, it's Colorado's highest and
steepest mountain pass on a major highway. On the

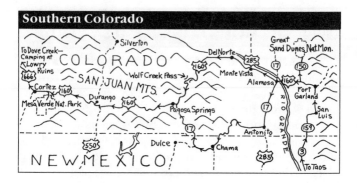

Southern Colorado

ascent, you may see (or join) numerous tourist vehicles overheated by the roadside. The long runaway truck ramp on the descent is there for a reason: be very careful not to "ride" your vehicle's brakes, which will overheat them and cause them to fail. This pass can pose a formidable obstacle to motor homes. Traffic may distract you from the scenery.

I suggest you try the much less traveled route over La Manga and Cumbres passes (10,230 feet and 10,022 feet). While these twin passes aren't much lower than Wolf Creek, the climb is more gradual. The relaxing drive through high mountain meadows is worth the extra 1½ hours of driving time. From Alamosa, turn left and follow US 285 straight south to Antonito (28 miles). Turn right (west) on State Highway 17 toward Chama. The highway climbs up from the San Luis Valley into San Juan National Forest, first following the Conejos River past a series of campgrounds and fishing spots, then ascending into the alpine meadows. At the top you'll see the tracks of the Cumbres & Toltec Scenic Railroad, which runs between Antonito and Chama by a different route. At the far end of the grassy slopes, just before you begin your descent, stand the train station, snowshed, and other abandoned buildings of Cumbres, a railroad ghost town from the 1880s. Descend into New Mexico. The road distance from Antonito to Chama is 48 miles.

At the junction about a mile south of Chama, just a few

miles over the state line, turn right on US 84, which climbs back up into the national forest to Pagosa Springs, Colorado, 49 miles away. There, rejoin US 160 westbound to Durango (60 miles). Mesa Verde National Park is 36 miles past Durango on US 160.

Durango

Durango, a lively town of about 12,000 people, got its start in 1880 as a rail hub serving local ranches as well as gold and silver mines in the mountains to the north. Today, Durango thrives on tourism. The downtown historic district, centered around the D&SNG railroad station and the Strater Hotel, has been prettified far beyond its original Victorian splendor. Besides being close to Mesa Verde, Durango attracts year-round tourism with its famous narrow gauge railroad, Purgatory ski area (which has an alpine slide in the summertime), the annual Iron Horse Bicycle Race, rafting, fishing, cross-country skiing, and a host of other outdoor recreation possibilities.

In recent years, Durango has attracted an impressive number of fine artists and craftsmen, whose creations can be seen in at least 15 galleries and shops on and near Main Avenue between Fifth and Eleventh streets. The Durango Arts Center at 970 Main Avenue (259-2606) exhibits works by local artists and serves as a ticket outlet for the performing arts in the area.

Camping

Morefield Campground in Mesa Verde National Park is located 5 miles up the steep road from the park entrance. It's a huge campground—177 tent sites, 300 trailer/RV sites. Besides all the usual campground amenities, there are pay showers nearby at the grocery store. Camping costs $7 plus park admission. Campfire programs are presented nightly. The Knife Edge Trail, which starts at the edge of the campground, takes you out to a cliff view point ideal for sunset watching. Returning in the dusk, you're likely to see dozens of deer grazing in the meadow.

If the campground at Mesa Verde is full or you'd prefer to sleep with fewer fellow campers around, at **Lowry Ruins Historic Site** you may find yourself all alone. Operated by the Bureau of Land Management, the site is not marked on most road maps and is known to only the most dedicated Indian ruins buffs. There is no admission or camping fee, no ranger on duty, and no water, so be sure you have plenty aboard. To get to Lowry Ruins, continue on US 160 10 miles beyond the Mesa Verde turnoff to the town of Cortez, and from there go north 19 miles on US 666 to Pleasant View, where a small road goes west (left) 9 miles to the ruins.

Lodging

Far View Motor Lodge is located in Mesa Verde National Park, midway along the park road near Far View Visitor Center. Rates are about $80, the views are magnificent, and there is a good restaurant at the lodge as well as a cafeteria at the visitors center. For current prices and reservations, contact ARA Mesa Verde Company, Box 277, Mancos, CO 81328, (303) 529-4421.

Durango has an abundance of hotels and motels in all price ranges. The finest is the **Strater Hotel**, the four-story brick centerpiece of downtown Durango's historic restoration district, at 699 Main Avenue. Dating back to 1887, the Strater has been undergoing room-by-room restoration for over 20 years. Guest rooms feature antique walnut furnishings, and public areas include a playhouse where melodramas are performed from June through September and an elegant Old West saloon. For reservations, call toll-free (800) 227-4431 in Colorado or (800) 247-4431 nationwide. Doubles start at $92.

Moderately priced motels are concentrated along North Main Avenue (US 550 northbound). Good bets are the **Caboose Motel**, 3363 N. Main Avenue, (303) 247-1191, with $34 to $48 doubles, and the **Alpine Motel**, 3515 N. Main Avenue, (303) 247-4042, which has $42 doubles.

Food

Durango has even more restaurants per capita than Santa Fe but no distinctive regional cuisine. Cruise the streets of town and pick a place that suits your mood. It costs less than you might expect to dine in an antique-filled Victorian atmosphere at **Henry's**, the Strater Hotel's restaurant. Steak or seafood dinners range between $10 and $20. It will be more than a week before you find another restaurant in the Southwest as splurge-worthy as this one.

Itinerary Options

If you have an extra day to spend in southwestern Colorado, consider a day trip on either of two restored narrow gauge railroads.

The **Cumbres & Toltec Scenic Railroad** runs between Antonito, Colorado, and Chama, New Mexico, along a different route than the highway described in the Travel Route above. The train runs round-trips departing at 10:00 a.m. daily May through mid-October from either town to the midpoint at Osier ($29 adult, $11 for children 11 and under), and one-way train trips for the full length of the route with return transportation by van (adults $45, children $23). Make reservations well in advance through the Antonito depot, P.O. Box 668, Antonito, CO 81120, (719) 376-5483, or the Chama depot, P.O. Box 789, Chama, NM 87520, (505) 756-2151.

The San Juan Mountains north of Durango, the most spectacular in the Colorado Rockies, bear a striking resemblance to the Swiss Alps. I wish I could fit them into this 22-day itinerary, but they're just too big. The **Durango & Silverton Narrow Gauge Railroad** runs between Durango and the old mining/ lumbering town of Silverton high in the mountains, round-trip only. It operates from mid-May through late September, departing daily at 8:30 and 9:30 a.m., returning at approximately 5:15 and 6:15 p.m., with additional departures during peak season. Fares are $37.15 for adults, $18.65 for children ages 5 to 11; there is also a Parlor Car, serving alcoholic beverages, with a higher fare of $63.85. The D&SNG is one of Colorado's most popular tourist attractions, and reservations should be made months in advance if possible. Contact D&SNG, 479 Main Avenue, Durango, CO 81301, (303) 247-2733.

The **Million Dollar Highway** (US 550, also called the San Juan Skyway), north from Durango through Silverton to Ouray, rivals the train trip for scenery. The road distance is 72 miles each way. It doesn't sound like far, but plan on an all-day trip. The highway is paved but steep and curvy. If you're traveling in a large motor home, you will find riding the D&SNG train to Silverton more relaxing and economical than driving.

You'll find complete details on touring the San Juan Mountains and the Durango region in this book's companion volume, *2 to 22 Days in the Rockies* by Roger Rapoport.

MESA VERDE

Today, you'll begin exploring the ruins left behind by the remote ancestors of the ancient and modern Pueblo Indians you saw in the Santa Fe-Los Alamos-Taos area. The Anasazi people thrived in the Four Corners area for seven centuries until, 800 years ago, they suddenly vanished from the region. Today, their monumental cliff dwellings at Mesa Verde are a popular, often crowded national park.

Suggested Schedule

9:00 a.m.	Drive to the museum on Chapin Mesa. (If you're staying in Durango rather than in Mesa Verde National Park, start an hour earlier.)
10:00 a.m.	Visit the museum and learn about the people who lived in these amazing cliff dwellings.
11:00 a.m.	Walk the trail behind the museum into Spruce Tree Canyon.
1:00 p.m.	Did you bring picnic supplies? If not, grab a quick bite at the snack bar near the museum or drive back to Far View Visitor Center, where there is a cafeteria.
Afternoon	Rent a bicycle at the museum for a leisurely tour of the cliff dwellings on Chapin Mesa, then finish your day with a hike from the museum out to Petroglyph Point. Or, the less athletic may wish to tour Chapin Mesa by car and then return to Far View Visitor Center for a drive out to Wetherill Mesa.
Evening	Spend a second night in the park or in Durango.

The Anasazi

"Anasazi" is a Navajo word meaning "ancestors of our enemies" (the National Park Service translates it more politely as "ancient ones"). It is the name given to the ancestors of the Pueblo Indians who lived in the Four Corners area until the twelfth century A.D. Of several distinct Anasazi groups, the three largest were the Mesa Verde and Chaco cultures, whose cities you'll see today and tomorrow, and the Kayenta people who built the cliff dwellings at Navajo National Monument (Day 9).

The Anasazi lived at the northernmost reach of trade routes established by the Toltecs and other great civilizations of Mexico, so they learned agricultural, architectural, and other technologies much earlier than did tribes in other parts of northern America. Their religion, too, evolved from Mexican origins. From about A.D. 1000 on, the Anasazi had the largest cities north of the tropics on the American continent.

In the twelfth century, within one or two generations, the Anasazi abandoned their pueblos one after another until the Four Corners area was virtually unpopulated. Nobody knows why. War? Disease? Drought? Wanderlust? Anthropologists argue endlessly. The current theory is that overpopulation brought soil depletion, erosion, and environmental disaster. The mysterious fall of the Anasazi empire is worthy of meditation among the ruins.

Mesa Verde National Park
In 1906, when Mesa Verde was made a national park to protect the largest and most extensive cliff dwellings in North America, the rare horseback visitor must have found the experience of a lifetime. Today its immense popularity, necessitating crowd control to protect archaeological sites, channels many tourists into a few public areas, making Mesa Verde a congested place. Yet the magic of this piñon-covered island 2,000 feet in the sky, with its ancient, castlelike "lost cities," makes itself felt even in a crowd.

Start touring Mesa Verde early in the morning to beat the charter buses. Admission to the park is $5 per vehicle. After a long, steep climb to the mesa top (travel trailers must be left below at the entrance station parking area or at the campground) and a pause at Park Point, with its superb view of the Mancos and Montezuma valleys and the San Juan Mountains, midway along the park road you'll come to Far View Visitor Center, where you can find out the current schedule for ranger-guided walks. One of these walks, offered free by the National Park Service, can enhance your Mesa Verde experience with insights about the people who once lived here and the plants and animals that still do.

Sightseeing Highlights

▲▲ Mesa Verde Museum—This old stone museum at park headquarters on Chapin Mesa, 20 miles from the park entrance, contains dioramas that show how civilization evolved on Mesa Verde during the same time period as Europe's Dark Ages. Take time to admire the museum's collection of ancient pottery, with its fine craftsmanship and elaborate geometric designs, and appreciate the thousand-year artistic heritage behind the Pueblo pottery you saw (and may have bought) in Albuquerque, Santa Fe, and Taos. The museum is open daily from 8:00 a.m. to 5:00 p.m., free.

▲▲▲ Chapin Mesa Ruins—Two separate loop roads begin at the museum on Chapin Mesa. Each road is about 3 miles round-trip and worth taking your time. Rent a bicycle at the museum, and the tour will seem even more spectacular. The major cliff dwellings are on the west loop, a left turn not far past the museum parking area. Of the many sites, Cliff Palace is the largest. It is accessible on a half-mile trail with a 500-foot climb; allow an hour. The walk to Balcony House, on the same road as it loops around to the other side of the mesa, means climbing a 32-foot ladder, ducking through a 12-foot tunnel, and ascending 100 feet up the cliff face. During crowded times, you can only see these two ruins on ranger-guided tours, which run frequently. The tour is well worth the wait.

▲▲ Walking Trails—If you want to escape the crowds at Mesa Verde, walk. Two trails begin at the museum, where you must obtain a free hiking permit. The permit system and many visitors' aversion to physical exercise keep the trails uncrowded—only one out of a thousand visitors hikes either trail. Spruce Canyon Trail is 2.1 miles long with a 700-foot climb down and back. Petroglyph Point Trail is 2.3 miles long with no steep climbing. Either takes about two hours round-trip.

▲ **Wetherill Mesa**—A 20-mile drive from the Far View Visitor Center leads to recently excavated mesa-top pueblo ruins. The area could only be reached by shuttle bus until recently but is now open to automobiles, a move the park service hopes will alleviate traffic congestion in the main ruins area on Chapin Mesa. Keep your eyes peeled for wild horses along the way.

AZTEC AND CHACO CANYON

Today's journey takes you to Anasazi ruins larger, more remote, and even more mysterious than those at Mesa Verde. If you are equipped to camp and have at least a day's worth of food aboard, you can take time to explore Chaco Canyon, the Southwest's premier Indian ruin, and let your imagination run free. (Otherwise, you'll have to speed up today's sightseeing in order to reach Interstate 40, where the nearest motels are, by nightfall.)

Suggested Schedule

9:30 a.m.	Drive south from Durango to Aztec. (Start an hour earlier if you spent last night at Mesa Verde National Park.)
10:00 a.m.	See Aztec Ruins National Monument.
11:30 a.m.	Drive to Angel Peak Recreation Area.
12:00 noon	Picnic.
1:00 p.m.	Drive to Chaco Canyon.
3:00 p.m.	Explore Chaco Canyon.
Evening	Camp at Chaco Canyon.

Travel Route: Mesa Verde to Aztec (71 miles)

From Mesa Verde National Park, return to Durango on US 160. Five miles east of Durango, where the highway forks, take US 550 south to Aztec. The total driving time from Mesa Verde to Aztec is 1½ hours.

The town of Aztec, population 6,000, won the National Municipal League's "All-American City" title in 1963 for building a 14-mile road to Navajo Lake—without help from any level of government. All funds, labor, and machinery were donated by local citizens. Aztec still takes the title to heart. A walk along the main street, with its small turn-of-the-century historic district and quaint local museum, can make you feel as if you'd slipped through time into Middle America, circa 1963.

Aztec Ruins National Monument is near the river, just

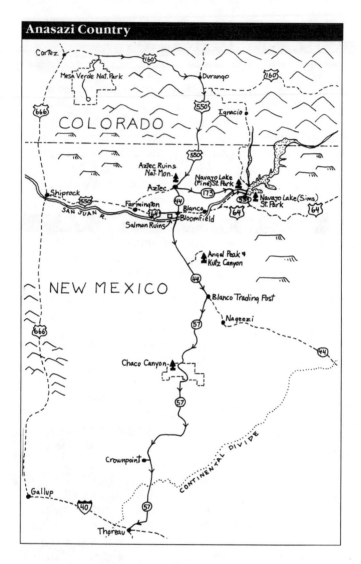

Anasazi Country

over the bridge from downtown Aztec on the road to Farmington, plainly marked with signs.

Aztec Ruins National Monument
Aztec Ruins, on the bank of the Animas River, was a large twelfth-century pueblo. Its name derives from early set-

tlers' mistaken belief that this and other southwestern
ruins were colonies from a higher civilization in Mexico.
While the Anasazi traded with Mexican Toltecs and perhaps Aztecs for parrots and other items, and some construction techniques apparently originated in Mexico,
Aztec was actually built by colonists from Chaco, 60
miles to the south. Abandoned during the decline of the
Chaco culture, the pueblo was later reoccupied by people
from Mesa Verde. Artifacts and architectural features from
both Anasazi cultures invite side-by-side comparison.
The showpiece of this national monument is the fully
reconstructed great kiva, which will help you appreciate
other kiva ruins, such as Chaco's Casa Rinconada, as prehistoric cathedrals, not just big holes in the ground. The
short (400-yard) path through the ruins is open from 8:00
a.m. to 5:00 p.m. daily all year and to 6:30 p.m. June
through August. Admission is $1 per adult, free for those
over 62 and under 17, or $3 per carload.

If these ruins fascinate you, consider a one-hour side
trip to Salmon Ruins, a similar Chacoan outlier pueblo
dating from the eleventh century, 12 miles from Aztec on
the road between Farmington and Bloomfield. Open 9:00
a.m. to 5:00 p.m. daily all year.

Travel Route: Aztec to Chaco Canyon (61 miles)

Fill up with gas and check your food supply before leaving Aztec; you won't see another town until tomorrow.
Drive south on NM 44 through the neighboring community of Bloomfield and out into the empty San Juan Basin.

Eighteen miles south of Aztec (13 miles past Bloomfield) on the left (east) is an unpaved road turnoff to
Angel Peak Recreation Area. Angel Peak itself is easy to
spot. It's the butte several miles to the east, crowned by
a rock formation that, with imagination, resembles an
angel with outspread wings. The sign marking the road
that takes you there is less obvious. Drive in just half a
mile to the first overlook and you'll be rewarded with a
totally unexpected view of Kutz Canyon, a bright bit of
red and white painted desert. There is a canyon rim picnic area 2 ½ miles farther down the road. A scenic free

campground 2 miles beyond that has 16 rarely used campsites with rest rooms, picnic tables and grills, but no
water.

Fifteen miles past the Angel Peak turnoff on NM 44 is
Blanco Trading Post, where a clearly marked road turns
off to the right (southwest) toward Chaco Culture National Historic Park. The road, unpaved and 30 miles
long, will take an hour to drive under good road conditions. "Don't pave the road to Chaco Canyon" was an
environmentalist rallying cry in the mid-1970s. The issue
of paving the road is coming around again in the 1990s as
Chaco Canyon becomes better known and more visited.
Still, while hordes of tourists overrun Mesa Verde, Chaco's
park rangers can usually relax with a few dozen adven-
turesome visitors. The road is normally an easy drive,
thrilling for a minute as it plunges headlong into the canyon to let you know you're almost there. If there have
been recent thunderstorms in the area, call Chaco headquarters, (505) 786-5384, for a road condition report
before proceeding. When wet, parts of the clay road can
be as slick as a skating pond.

The surrounding land is sparsely inhabited by Navajo
people. While not officially part of the reservation, most
ranches in the area have been purchased by the tribe and
are regarded as part of the Navajo Nation. There is no
gasoline, food, lodging, or repair service at Chaco, and
the nearest town is the one you just came from, 60 miles
away.

Chaco Culture National Historic Park
Until 1983, this site was called Chaco Canyon National
Monument. Its new tongue twister name notwithstand-
ing, most folks still just call it Chaco Canyon.

At Mesa Verde and Aztec, we can wonder why the
Anasazi suddenly abandoned such beautiful spots. Chaco
presents different archaeological mysteries. With so
much wide open space around, why did the Chacoans
cluster together into a mega-pueblo, the largest city the
Anasazi ever saw, the Los Angeles of the prehistoric

Southwest? And why, of all places, here?

Even with its sophisticated irrigation system, Chacoans could not grow enough food to support the population of 5,000 but had to import it from outlier colonies. For vigas, or roof and floor supports in the pueblos, the people had to carry countless thousands of ponderosa logs from the mountains fifty miles away, a formidable task considering that they had no horses, nor had they knowledge of the wheel. Chacoans' abundant turquoise supply came from even farther away, in the Cerrillos hills near Santa Fe. While they made elaborate and distinctive black-on-white decorative pottery, most everyday cooking pots were imported. What did they give in exchange for all the imports needed to keep this city alive?

Archaeologists don't know. A clue may lie in the extraordinary number of kivas at Chaco, which suggest that it was a religious center. Natural beauty, the spirit of place, was probably important in the religion of the Anasazi, as it is to their Pueblo descendants today. Especially at twilight, one can readily imagine Chaco Canyon as sacred land.

The largest pueblo, Pueblo Bonito, rose four stories and contained 800 rooms. Besides all the excavated pueblos you see here, there are a number of others in the area that are crumbled and buried, recognizable only by differing vegetation. The Chaco people also established about 60 satellite pueblos called "outliers" throughout the San Juan Basin, from Aztec in the north to the Grants area in the south. The major outliers were connected by an 800-mile network of improved roads thirty feet wide, with Chaco at the hub.

Late afternoon or early morning is the best time to tour and photograph the ruins. For solitude and a different perspective on Chaco Canyon, hike the trail up to Tsin Kletsin ruins (4-mile, 2½-hour round-trip) on the canyon rim. The trail starts at Casa Rinconada, Chaco's largest great kiva.

Chaco Canyon is open year-round (road conditions permitting). No admission is charged.

Camping
Chaco's **Gallo Campground** is small, with only about
two dozen established sites. A sign on the road into the
park warns that the campground may fill up by 3:00 p.m.
In fact, the park has become so popular in the last few
years that the campground overflows almost every night,
even off-season. Campers who arrive too late to obtain a
site are permitted to park along a nearby gravel road—
fine if you're in a self-contained RV, but a little rugged if
you're pitching a tent. The campground has tables, fireplaces, and rest rooms. The only water supply is at the
visitors center, about half a mile away. Rangers present
campfire programs nightly during the summer season.

Lodging
The closest motels to Chaco Canyon are in the Farming-
ton-Bloomfield-Aztec area and the Grants-Gallup area,
each two hours away. The only campground is the one in
the park. Bring your own food.

Itinerary Option
If you have extra time and a yearning for water, head for
Navajo Lake, New Mexico's largest lake, near Aztec. Pine
River Marina, 23 miles east of Aztec on NM 511 not far
above the dam, has the nearest campground and boat
rental. More remote facilities are at Sims Mesa across the
lake: turn left at the first fork in the road after you cross
the dam. Empty except on weekends, when the lake has
been known to attract as many as 7,500 visitors at a time!
Navajo Lake is a good place to rent a motorboat for a day
or overnight back-canyon boat-camping trip. A 40-
horsepower outboard rents for $10 an hour or $40 for 24
hours. A Kayot, a motorized raft with a roof which can
carry four to six people, costs $20 an hour or $80 for 24
hours.

CHACO CANYON TO CANYON DE CHELLY

Leaving Chaco Canyon by a different unpaved road, you'll return to I-40 just two hours' drive from Albuquerque, where you started nearly a week ago. Then begin your tour of the largest Indian reservation in the United States with a visit to the tribal zoo and historic Hubbell Trading Post. You'll end the day at Canyon de Chelly, the heart of the land of the Navajo.

Suggested Schedule

9:00 a.m.	Leave Chaco Canyon.
11:00 a.m.	Take a break in Gallup. Fill the gas tank, stock up on food.
11:30 a.m.	Visit Navajo Tribal Zoological Park.
12:30 p.m.	Picnic at Window Rock Tribal Park.
1:15 p.m.	Drive to Ganado.
2:00 p.m.	See Hubbell Trading Post.
3:15 p.m.	Drive to Canyon de Chelly National Monument.
4:00 p.m.	Arrive at Canyon de Chelly, find a campsite or check into the lodge, and visit the visitors center.
5:00 p.m.	Take a late afternoon drive along the north rim of Canyon del Muerto.

Travel Route: Chaco Canyon to Canyon de Chelly (156 miles)

The road south out of Chaco Canyon doesn't take as long to reach the pavement—just 10 dusty miles. Continue south and west on NM 57 as it joins the Vietnam Veterans Memorial Highway near Crownpoint and, 32 miles later, reaches I-40 at the tiny town of Thoreau, midway between Grants and Gallup.

Take the interstate west for 33 miles to Gallup (pop. 20,000), the "border town" of the Navajo Nation. Existing primarily as a truck stop and railroad way station, Gallup has an old downtown area on the south side of the

Navajoland

interstate and train tracks and a strip of shopping malls,
supermarkets, and fast-food places on the north side. On
the old side, pawn shops, curio shops, and trading companies sell Navajo and Zuñi arts and crafts at prices far
lower than those in Albuquerque or Santa Fe. Some of the
turn-of-the-century storefronts along Main Street have
had recent face lifts to become galleries, but Gallup is a
long way from becoming a touristy historic district.
Restaurants and motels are, on the whole, budget-basic.
Drunken Indians are a common sight at any time of day
or night. Draw no general conclusions about Native
Americans from encounters with these few; it's just that
Gallup is the only place in the region where a man can
get a drink if he craves one. Alcoholic beverages are illegal
on the Navajo Reservation and hard to get beyond the
reservation's northern boundary, in Utah, where anything
stronger than beer is only sold in state liquor stores

whose locations often seem like closely guarded secrets.

Take four-lane US 666 north from Gallup for 7 miles and turn west on Highway 264 to Window Rock, the Navajo Nation's capital (pop. 2,200). You will cross the Arizona state line shortly before entering town. Although the rest of Arizona stays on Mountain Standard Time while New Mexico, Colorado, and Utah observe daylight saving time, the entire Navajo Nation also goes on daylight saving time, so there is no need to reset your watch on this leg of the trip. (In fact, for the next few days there will be very little reason to consult your watch at all.)

From Window Rock, continue on Highway 264 for 34 more miles to reach Hubbell Trading Post, a mile past Ganado near the intersection with US 191. After visiting the trading post, turn north on US 191 and drive 31 miles to the turnoff for Chinle and Canyon de Chelly National Monument.

The Navajo Nation

The Navajo Nation encompasses nearly 16 million acres, an area larger than Connecticut, Massachusetts, and New Hampshire combined. The eastern part of the reservation is mountainous evergreen forest with several recreation lakes; the center is the arid, piñon-covered Lukachukai Plateau; and the western part is painted desert. All land on the reservation is inhabited, a fact that is not obvious because the Navajo traditionally locate each house out of sight of any other house.

Athabascan Indians migrated from northwestern Canada to New Mexico and Arizona shortly before the Spanish did. Those who adopted new ways from the Pueblo people and Spanish settlers, such as sheepherding, weaving, and growing corn, came to be called Navajo (from a Pueblo word meaning "green planted fields"). The other Athabascans, who held to their older nomadic traditions, were called Apache.

In 1864, soon after the Navajo lands became U.S. territory (most reservation Navajo, young and old alike, talk as though it happened yesterday), Kit Carson's army burned the Navajo cornfields to starve the people out of hiding.

Carson then marched the Navajo people, who then num-
bered about 8,000, along with 2,000 horses and 10,000
sheep and goats, for 300 miles to a camp at Fort Sumner
in eastern New Mexico. Without supplies, many Navajo
died along the trail. Famine plagued the Fort Sumner
camps; meanwhile, American surveyors could find nothing desirable about the former Navajo lands. Four years
later, the army marched the remaining Navajo and their
flocks back home. The degrading experience fostered
tribal unity, increased distrust of the white man, height-
ened belief in the special quality of their homeland, and
galvanized the "Navajo Nation."

In a few scattered towns, twentieth-century con-
veniences such as pickup trucks, video rental stores, and
government housing projects adorned by satellite TV
antennas—new additions to the tribe's unique way of
life—have all been borrowed from the American mainstream. Horses, sheep, corn, jewelry making, and weaving were all similarly borrowed to create the traditional
Navajo life-style, and the process continues.

The more you travel in Navajoland, the more it may
seem like a Third World country (though one with exceptional respect for the natural environment). Most Navajo
people live away from towns and highways and have no
electricity or running water. The tribe faces problems of
poverty and overpopulation. The Navajo Nation, the
largest tribe in the United States, now numbers about
200,000. Only 20 percent can live off the land, and of the
rest, 85 percent are unemployed. Coal mines and natural
gas wells provide tribal income and a few jobs but scar
the land. Experimental reservation industries range from
a pilot microchip plant (now closed) to cultivation of rare
oriental mushrooms.

You'll see signs on the reservation for three kinds of
places important in Navajo society—trading posts, chapterhouses, and missions.

Trading posts are general stores operated by traders
under federal license. They sell a selection of food some-
what more limited than 7-Eleven stores, as well as dry
goods, gasoline, and sometimes hay or feed for livestock.

Traditionally, traders also served as pawnbrokers, exchanging their wares for rugs and jewelry that they sold to collectors, and some trading posts continue the practice. If you stop at enough trading posts, you'll find a fair selection of Navajo handicrafts. For many Navajo it's a long trip to the trading post, and once there, they like to stay around for a good part of the day, talking with whoever else stops by.

Chapterhouses are the basic unit of Navajo tribal government. They serve the purpose of town meeting halls, even though many are far from any town. Chapters elect 88 councilmen to represent them in the tribal council. The Council Chambers, near Window Rock Tribal Park, are open from 8:00 a.m. to 5:00 p.m. on many weekdays. Visitors fortunate enough to find the council in session will hear tribal issues debated in both English and Navajo.

Missions have been established throughout the reservation by a number of Christian denominations. The first, at Ganado, was built by the Presbyterians under a decree from President Grant which arbitrarily assigned Indian reservations to various missionary groups. Since the beginning of the twentieth century, other missionaries have included the Franciscan Order and the Methodist and Christian Reformed churches. Visitors are welcome at all of them. Christian fundamentalist tent revivals, too, are held frequently around the reservation. Some feature Navajo preachers. If you come across one (audible for miles, they're hard to miss), by all means join the flock. Old-time evangelism among the Indians makes for a unique and thought-provoking cultural experience regardless of your personal faith. Traditional Navajo religious beliefs survive, and "sings"—healing ceremonies that involve chanting and sand painting—still take place, though non-Navajo visitors are rarely included.

Sightseeing Highlights
▲▲ Navajo Tribal Zoological Park—This low-budget zoo looks like a combination barnyard and humane society shelter, but don't let first impressions put you off. Here you'll feel the Navajo people's unique attitude to-

ward animals. Sheep and other domestic animals roam throughout the grounds, while wild animals (most were found injured and brought here from other parts of the reservation) are kept in wire pens to protect them from tourists. Signs name each animal in both English and Navajo, and a display in the visitors center tells a little bit about the animals' mythological roles as spiritual fore-fathers of the various Navajo clans. Among the zoo's residents are a black bear, a mountain lion, a wolf, birds of prey, and sometimes bison. Located off Arizona 264, a half-mile east of Window Rock Shopping Center, the zoo is open daily from 8:00 a.m. to 5:00 p.m.; 50 cents per person donation requested.

▲ **Navajo Tribal Museum**—Exhibits depict Navajo history. There are also Anasazi artifacts and a large arts and crafts shop. On Arizona 264 between the shopping center and Window Rock Motor Inn, the museum is open Monday through Friday, 8:00 a.m. to 5:00 p.m. Donations are welcome.

▲ **Window Rock Tribal Park**—The rock formation for which the Navajo capital was named is ½ mile east (right) off Tribal Route 12, ½ mile north of Arizona 264. There are picnic tables, rest rooms, water, and a walking trail.

▲▲ **Hubbell Trading Post National Historic Site**—John Lorenzo Hubbell, the New Mexico-born son of a U.S. soldier, founded this trading post in 1878. It became the center of his Navajo Reservation trade empire, which grew to include 24 trading posts as well as stage and freight lines. Arriving among the Navajo soon after the second Long Walk, as the people were struggling to adjust to reservation life, Hubbell served as the Indians' spokesman and contact with the white world for over 50 years. He wrote, "The first duty of an Indian trader is to advise them to produce that which their natural inclinations and talent best adapts them, to find a market for their products and vigilantly watch that they keep improving in the production of same, and advise them which commands the best price." Hubbell encouraged the Navajo to develop the high-quality rug weaving and silversmithing for which they are known today.

Hubbell Trading Post, the oldest continuously active trading post on the reservation, still sells food and dry goods to the Indians and excellent-quality Navajo goods to tourists. Weavers and silversmiths demonstrate their arts at the visitors center. Take a free guided tour of Hubbell's home and grounds. Both the trading post and the visitors center are open daily from 8:00 a.m. to 6:00 p.m. in the summer, 8:00 a.m. to 5:00 p.m. the rest of the year. Admission is free.

▲▲▲ **Canyon de Chelly National Monument: North Rim (Canyon del Muerto)**—Taking the north rim drive this evening and seeing the south rim—which is a different canyon—tomorrow morning will let you make the most of the fairly limited automobile sightseeing possibilities at Canyon de Chelly National Monument. The overlooks along the two scenic drives afford the only views you get of Canyon de Chelly and Canyon del Muerto unless you take a horseback trip into the canyon with a Navajo guide (see "Itinerary Options"). Traditional Navajo herdsmen live in hogans below the sheer, impassable cliffs, seemingly oblivious to the tourists who daily peer down at them from the rim. To explore the canyon, use binoculars.

Canyon de Chelly (the name, pronounced "d'SHAY," is an Anglo mispronunciation of a Spanish misspelling of *Tsegi*, Navajo for "rock canyon") is the traditional center of the Navajo lands. According to their mythology, the Navajo people and animals emerged into the world from this place.

Canyon de Chelly National Monument headquarters area has a visitors center (open daily, 8:00 a.m. to 6:00 p.m. May through September, 8:00 a.m. to 5:00 p.m. October through April), campground, and lodge. There is no admission fee to Canyon de Chelly. Various brochures available at the visitors center cost fifty cents each. Tribal Road 64 goes from the park headquarters area to the small Navajo college town of Tsaile, 35 miles away, but sightseers need only drive the first 18 miles to see all the view points along the north rim of Canyon del Muerto, then return by the same route. Five miles up the road from the visitors center is Ledge Ruin Viewpoint, an unexcavated Anasazi ruin that had about fifty rooms and two kivas. Three miles farther up the road is Antelope House Overlook, named for the paintings of antelope on the canyon wall to the left of the ruin, probably painted by a Navajo artist in the early nineteenth century. Nearby paintings of hands and other figures are from the Anasazi people who lived here as early as the seventh century.

Ten more miles up the road will bring you to a turnoff on your right (south) to Mummy Cave and Massacre Cave overlooks. Mummy Cave is the site of one of the largest Anasazi ruins in the canyon, a 77-room, Mesa Verde-style cliff dwelling with a three-story tower. Discovery in the 1880s of two mummies buried at this site gave the canyon its name (which means "Canyon of the Dead"). Massacre Cave was so named because a Spanish expedition slaughtered 115 Indians here in 1805.

Camping

Canyon de Chelly's **Cottonwood Campground**, half a mile from the visitors center, has rest rooms, picnic tables, water, and a dumping station but no hookups or showers. Camping is free. Rangers present campfire programs nightly during the summer months.

Lodging

Rooms at Canyon de Chelly's **Thunderbird Lodge**, near the visitors center and campground, range from $84 to $89 double ($10 less off-season). For reservations, call (602) 674-5841. **Canyon de Chelly Motel**, 1½ miles away on the outskirts of Chinle, has rooms for $78. Call (602) 674-5875.

Food

The cafeteria at **Thunderbird Lodge**, open 7:00 a.m. to 8:30 p.m., serves good food at moderate prices. Try a Navajo taco—Indian-style fry bread heaped with meat, beans, lettuce, and cheese. Although $5 might sound like a high price for a taco, this one will fill you up with some left over. Navajo sand paintings displayed in the cafeteria are among the finest you'll see anywhere.

Nearby, Chinle has a shopping center with a supermarket as well as two local cafés and a **Kentucky Fried Chicken**.

Helpful Hints

Tourist brochures warn that traditional Navajo may refuse to talk to non-Indian tourists, but my experience has been that most people on the reservation are quite willing to talk with outsiders. What may seem like shyness or unfriendliness is actually cultural difference: Navajo people are taught from childhood not to talk too much, be loud, or start conversations with strangers, and eye contact while speaking is considered impolite. A good way to meet an Indian who doesn't work in the tourist trade is to offer a ride to a hitchhiker. It's safe (but use discretion on the highway from Gallup to Window Rock). Hitching rides is common on the reservation, because there is no public transportation.

While a few older people on the reservation speak no English, nearly all Navajo, young and old alike, are bilingual. Despite early attempts by the U.S. government to eradicate it through boarding school education, the Navajo language is now a source of patriotic and tribal pride thanks largely to the "Code-talkers," 1,500 Navajo men who broadcast secret military messages among Pacific islands during World War II. Navajo was the only American "code" the Japanese never succeeded in deciphering. Listen to spoken Navajo as you drive across the reservation. Several area radio stations have Navajo-language programming at different times throughout the day. Try KTNN Window Rock, 660 on your AM radio dial.

Free camping or driving on back roads is a bad idea on the Navajo Reservation. Any time you leave the pavement, you're trespassing on somebody's grazing land, and back roads are usually somebody's driveway. Back roads on the reservation are often in terrible condition, easy to get stuck or lost on. Never enter a hogan or other home uninvited. If you need help, observe Navajo tradition and stop at least 50 yards away, call, then wait until someone comes out to see what you want. Respect for privacy helps ensure that the tribe will continue to welcome visitors.

Two major Native American events take place in the Gallup/Window Rock area in the late summer, and either is worth planning your trip around. The Inter-Tribal Ceremonial and Rodeo, the largest Indian powwow in the nation, takes place Thursday through Sunday the second weekend in August at Red Rocks State Park near Gallup; call (505) 863-3896 for complete information. The Navajo Nation Fair, the Navajo equivalent of a state fair with contest dancing, a rodeo, concerts, carnival rides, and a large, fascinating arts and crafts pavilion, is held Thursday through Sunday of the week following Labor Day. Since it is held on the same weekend as Santa Fe's much better known Fiesta, hardly any non-Indian tourists are among the 80,000 people who visit the Navajo Nation Fair each year.

Itinerary Options
Visitors are only allowed down into Canyon de Chelly or Canyon del Muerto when accompanied by Navajo guides, to protect the ancient ruins, the present-day residents' privacy, and you (from quicksand and flash floods), but you can arrange guided tours. The most exciting option is a one-day horseback trip up-canyon to Mummy Cave or Antelope House, $50 per person. Call **Twin Trail Tours** at (602) 871-4663 for information and reservations, or inquire at the visitors center. Four-wheel-drive tours can be arranged at **Thunderbird Lodge** for about $35 for a half day or $50 for a full day. Navajo guides to accompany you up-canyon on a hike or in your own four-wheel-drive vehicle can be arranged through **Tsegi Guide Association** at the visitors center, $9 per hour.

CANYON DE CHELLY TO MONUMENT VALLEY

For a close-up look at traditional Navajo life, drive from Canyon de Chelly in the heart of the Navajo Nation toward the reservation's northern boundary on the edge of Utah's uninhabited slickrock country and visit Monument Valley Tribal Park.

Suggested Schedule

8:00 a.m.	Breakfast.
9:00 a.m.	Canyon de Chelly south rim drive.
10:30 a.m.	Drive to Kayenta.
11:30 a.m.	Drive to Navajo National Monument. Picnic and see Betatakin ruins.
2:00 p.m.	Drive to Monument Valley.
3:30 p.m.	Explore Monument Valley.
5:00 p.m.	Camp at Monument Valley or stay at Goulding's Trading Post.

Travel Route: Chinle to Monument Valley (104 miles)
Leaving Canyon de Chelly, take US 191 north from Chinle for 15 miles to the barely noticeable community of Many Farms, and turn left (west) there on Tribal Route 59. A 58-mile drive along the base of Black Mesa will bring you to US 160. Turn left (west again) and go 8 miles to Kayenta. To visit Navajo National Monument, continue west on US 160 for 22 miles, then go 9 miles north on Arizona 564. After visiting Navajo National Monument, retrace your route back to Kayenta. From Kayenta to Monument Valley is 23 miles via US 163.

Sightseeing Highlights
▲▲▲ **Canyon de Chelly National Monument: South Rim**—Take the 22-mile (each way) scenic drive from the visitors center along the south rim of the canyon. Tsegi Overlook, 2.5 miles along the road, affords an excellent

view of traditional hogans and farms on the canyon floor, and 1.4 miles beyond that is Junction Overlook, where you can see two early Anasazi ruins. Two miles farther on is White House Overlook; about 150 yards to the right of the overlook is the only nonguided hiking trail into Canyon de Chelly, a two-hour, 2½-mile round-trip, 500-foot descent to the large White House Ruin. Bring water. Fifteen miles from there, at the upper end of the canyon, is the overlook for Spider Rock, a solitary 800-foot pinnacle on top of which, according to legend, Spider Woman lives. Not a comic book character, Spider Woman is the mythological being who taught Navajo women the art of weaving. Spider Rock is the last stop on the south rim scenic drive. Return to the visitors center the same way you came.

▲ **Navajo National Monument**—The monument protects major cliff dwellings of the Kayenta culture, the third major Anasazi group (the others being the Chaco and Mesa Verde cultures). The only easily accessible ruin is Betatakin, which can be seen from the easy one-mile trail that starts at the visitors center. If you have extra time, consider a guided 16-mile wilderness hike or horseback trip into the backcountry to see Keet Seel, the largest cliff dwelling in Arizona and one of the best preserved anywhere. Keet Seel was occupied for only 25 years, yet centuries later, charcoal remains in the hearths, and there are dried ears of corn in the grain storage rooms. For information and reservations, contact Navajo National Monument, H.C. 63, Box 3, Tonalea, AZ 86044, (602) 672-2366. Horseback trips cost about $50 per person. The number of visitors to Keet Seel is limited to 25 per day, so make reservations well in advance.

▲▲▲ **Monument Valley Navajo Tribal Park**—A combination of strange landscape, traditional Navajo life, and sincere if humble tribal hospitality gives the valley a special quality that is unrivaled. As you overlook Monument Valley from the visitors center, you may be struck by déjà vu. This desert landscape, with its spirelike buttes and mesas, has been background scenery for so many Western movies, TV shows, and commercials that you'll recognize it instantly. John Ford's Point is named after the director of *Stagecoach* (1938), the first motion picture ever filmed here.

Taking the 17-mile unpaved road through the valley seems like driving through a movie, too. Along the way you'll discover the real magic of Monument Valley: people live here. This is not an open-air folk museum, and the people have not been hired to look picturesque for tourists. Their families happened to live here when Monument Valley became a tribal park in 1958, and they still do. Of approximately 100 Navajo who make their homes in Monument Valley, most are descendants of families who fled here a century ago to escape the Long March.

Today, Monument Valley residents thrive on tourism. Even with nearly a million visitors a year, the quiet curio business makes a delightful counterpoint to high-pressure hype encountered in places such as Las Vegas. Many things still cost only a dollar, though worth far more. Beside one roadside ramada where a twelve-year-old Navajo girl offers cedar-bead necklaces, a sign handwritten on cardboard reads: "Beads and rug for sale. Taken picture of the girls or woman weaving you pay them $1.00 each for each of them. look inside hogan is $1.00 per person and taken pix of hogans $1.00 too. Thanx."

A guided tour is worthwhile in Monument Valley, since some roads are for four-wheel-drive tour vehicles only. Of several tours available at the visitors center, I recommend Navajo Guided Tour Service, the only company whose owner-operators were born and raised in Monument Valley. All of their tours cover the same 28-mile backcountry route, including Anasazi ruins, petroglyphs, and a visit to the guide's grandmother's hogan. Longer trips proceed at a slower pace. Two-hour trips run $20/person; half-day, $25/person; full-day, $40/person including lunch. Plus $1 per person ($0.50 for kids) for the grandmother. Sunrise and sunset trips cost slightly more. For more information, contact Frank or Linda Rodriguez, 450 East Pinion Road, #7, Blanding, UT 84511,

(801) 678-2360. Monument Valley's visitors center and
scenic drive are open from 7:00 a.m. to 8:00 p.m. May
through September, 8:00 a.m. to 5:00 p.m. October
through April. Admission is $2.50 per adult, $1 for adults
over 62, free for children under 6.

Camping

Monument Valley has a 100-site campground that, according to officials there, is never full. The camping fee is
$7 plus park admission. The campsites are small and
close together, but there is boundless open space for evening desert walking nearby. Best of all, the central rest
rooms have pay showers.

Lodging

Goulding's Lodge and Trading Post, (801) 727-3231,
is in the opposite direction from the Monument Valley
entrance gate, two miles west of US 163. The historic
trading post has been operated by the same family for
almost seventy years. Rooms run $88 a night during tour-
ist season, as low as $52 off-season. Goulding's also has a
grocery store, a service station, and good-quality Navajo
handicrafts.

TRAIL OF THE ANCIENTS TO CANYONLANDS

Escalante National Park was proposed by conservationists in the 1930s. The plan was rejected. If it had passed, it would have protected over 7,000 square miles of southern Utah in one of the nation's largest parks. Though some of the land has been lost under the water of Lake Powell, many sightseeing highlights of would-be Escalante National Park are now state parks, national monuments, or national parks in their own right. Tour them today and tomorrow. Take the Trail of the Ancients north to Moab, Utah. Camp tonight on the Island in the Sky in the center of Canyonlands National Park, and explore Arches National Park this afternoon or tomorrow morning.

Suggested Schedule

8:00 a.m.	Drive to Natural Bridges National Monument.
9:30 a.m.	Natural Bridges scenic drive and hike.
11:30 a.m.	Drive to Blanding.
12:30 p.m.	Picnic at Devil's Canyon.
1:30 p.m.	Drive to Monticello.
2:00 p.m.	Drive to Moab.
4:00 p.m.	Drive to Canyonlands.
5:00 p.m.	Explore Island in the Sky. Camp at Canyonlands or Dead Horse Point, or spend the night in Moab.

Travel Route: Monument Valley to Natural Bridges (64 miles)

From Monument Valley, go northeast on US 163 for 26 miles, passing through the small town of Mexican Hat, Utah, on the Navajo Reservation boundary line. Just north of town on your right you'll see the town's namesake—a rock formation that looks like an upside-down sombrero.

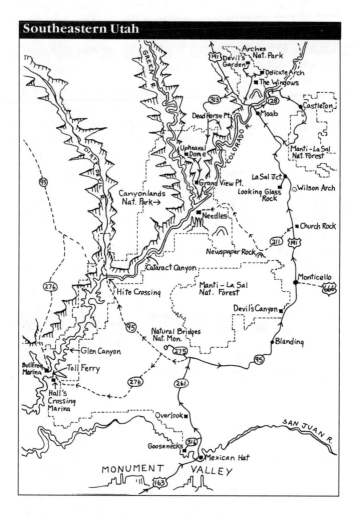

Southeastern Utah

Soon after you pass the hat, turn left (west) on UT 261,
known as the Trail of the Ancients.

Two scenic overlooks on the San Juan River, each a
short drive from the highway, deserve a look, especially if
you're recording your trip with photographs. Goose-
necks State Reserve (three-quarters of a mile from where
you turned onto UT 261, left 4 miles on a paved road, $3
entrance fee) affords a close-up view of 1,500-foot-deep

entrenched river meanders. Six miles farther north, a
4-mile unpaved road on your left goes to Muley Point,
with a broader view of the river's labyrinth and an
interpretive display on the area's geology; free, no facilities. Twenty-four miles north on UT 261 from the Muley
Point turnoff, you'll come to UT 95. Turn left (west), and
in less than a mile you'll reach the turnoff on your right to
Natural Bridges.

Natural Bridges National Monument

Tour Natural Bridges National Monument on the paved
8-mile scenic loop drive. The three natural bridges are
located in two adjacent canyons, with a hiking trail to
each one from the scenic loop. Owachomo Bridge is an
easy half-mile hike, while Sipapu and Kachina bridges are
each reached by a steep 1½-mile trail. Afternoon temperatures in the summer often reach 100 degrees, so if you'd
like to hike either of the longer trails, start early and plan
to complete your hike before noon. The monument also
has Anasazi cliff dwellings and pictographs. The visitors
center (open 8:00 a.m. to 4:30 p.m.) relies entirely on
solar electricity. In 1980, when it was built, it was the
largest photovoltaic system on earth. Admission to the
monument is $3 per vehicle.

Travel Route: Natural Bridges to Moab (108 miles)

Drive east from Natural Bridges on UT 95 a distance of 32
miles to Blanding. Along the way, a well-marked half-mile
dirt road to the right (south) goes to Cave Towers, seven
Anasazi fortress towers used in the eleventh and twelfth
centuries to defend a permanent underground spring in a
cave below. If you are driving a low-clearance vehicle, the
best plan for seeing this ruin is to park near the highway
and walk up the dirt road, about an hour round-trip.
There is also a short hiking trail to Indian ruins from
the Butler Wash rest area. The easy 1-mile, half-hour
round-trip trail goes to an overlook from which numerous ruins can be seen. Join US 191 northbound (left) into
Blanding. Just south of town, 2⅓ miles from the junc-

tion, a paved access road on the left goes to Westwater Ruin, yet another cliff dwelling. If you dare, cross Westwater Canyon on the swinging bridge to see a small natural bridge.

In Blanding, Edge of the Cedars State Historical Monument has a group of small pueblos and kivas, some dating back to A.D. 700. The ruins themselves are not outstanding, but the museum is. Open 9:00 a.m. to 6:00 p.m. during the summer months, until 5:00 p.m. the rest of the year. Admission is $1 per adult, $0.50 for children ages 6 to 15.

Continue north from Blanding on US 191. Four miles north is Devil's Canyon Campground, a good picnic stop. Drive all the way to the end of the campground, where you'll find a short (400 yard) trail to the rim of a canyon that thwarted pioneers and road builders for generations. It's 21 miles from Blanding to the town of Monticello, 55 more miles to Moab, all scenic. Fifteen miles before Moab, on the right, is the improbable Hole n'' the Rock Home, a 5,000-square-foot dwelling carved into the red sandstone cliff by the late Albert and Gladys Christensen between 1945 and 1957, still run by their family as a gift and rock shop. If the stone bust of Franklin D. Roosevelt that Albert carved into the cliff face intrigues you, tour the home and see 14 rooms arranged around large pillars. The fireplace has a 65-foot chimney drilled through solid rock. Open 9:00 a.m. to 6:00 p.m. during the summer months, until 5:00 p.m. the rest of the year. Admission is $2 for adults, $1 for children ages 5 to 12.

Moab

Moab (pop. 5,000) was a boomtown in the 1950s, when uranium prospecting along the Colorado River was big business. While other uranium towns have practically vanished from the map, Moab has flourished as a tourist town thanks to two new national parks nearby, Arches and Canyonlands. This is the place to fill up on gas and stock up on food and water.

During July and August, early afternoon in both Arches and Canyonlands is likely to be very hot. It's best to drive out to Canyonlands late in the afternoon, when you won't have to wait long for evening's coolness. In the meantime, you might drive the 60-mile LaSal Mountain Loop into cool mountain forests. Go north from Moab on US 191 and turn right onto UT 128 just before the bridge. Follow the Colorado River along the boundary of Arches National Park for 16 miles and take the turnoff to Castle Valley. Go south through Castle Valley 11 miles to the LaSal Mountain Loop Road turnoff on your right, which takes you into the national forest. The loop road will eventually bring you back to US 191 south of Moab. All but one mile of the route is paved.

When it comes to indoor sightseeing, Moab boasts the Hollywood Stuntmen's Hall of Fame and Museum (111 E. 100 North Street, 259-6100), where you can see equipment used in movie stunts as well as film clips of the motion picture industry's most remarkable accomplishments in stunts. Open April through September Monday through Friday from 12:00 noon to 9:00 p.m., Saturday and Sunday from 12:00 noon to 6:00 p.m. Admission is $3 for adults, $2 for students ages 12 to 18, and $1 for children ages 6 to 11.

A block south of the stuntmen's museum, the Dan O'Laurie Moab Museum (118 E. Center Street, 259-7985) features geological samples and dinosaur fossils to help you comprehend the area's complex landscapes. There are also Indian artifacts from the days when the Ute people lived around Moab and relics of Spanish and United States explorations in the area, as well as pioneer antiques. Open Monday through Saturday from 1:00 to 4:00 p.m. and 7:00 to 9:00 p.m. during the summer months, with more limited hours off-season. Admission is free.

If you are visiting the area during the cooler fall or spring months, skip the mountains and spend the afternoon seeing Arches National Park or arrive earlier at Canyonlands.

Canyonlands National Park: Island in the Sky

Be sure you have plenty of gas, food, and water before
leaving Moab.

The turnoff to Island in the Sky is to the left off US 191,
about 11 miles northwest of Moab, 6 miles past the Arches
National Park turnoff. It's 22 miles from the highway to
the park entrance. Stop and check in at the ranger sta-
tion/visitors center, just past The Neck, a ridge no wider
than the road, which is the only way on or off the
"island."

Stewart Udall, President Kennedy's Secretary of the
Interior, was surveying the site of a proposed dam on the
Colorado River above Cataract Canyon from a small plane
when he exclaimed, "My God, that's a national park
down there!" Two years later, in 1964, Canyonlands
National Park became a reality. If your idea of a national
park is the Grand Canyon, Yellowstone, or Yosemite, the
visitors center (in a converted mobile home) should tip
you off that Canyonlands is different. Its 337,570 acres,
sliced in thirds by the confluence of the Colorado and
Green rivers, contain some of the least accessible land
known to man. Most can only be reached by horseback,
raft, or four-wheel drive; some can't be reached at all.

Island in the Sky is a long, narrow promontory
between the two rivers, rising 2,000 feet above them. The
recently paved roads fork at Green River Overlook, 7
miles past the entrance, and go to opposite ends of the
12-mile-long "island." At the south tip, Grandview
Point affords a "look but don't touch" view from the
exact center of Canyonlands National Park. Explore with
binoculars and let your imagination roam over the mar-
velously complex landscape.

The White Rim is 1,000 feet below, midway down to
river level. Look carefully and you may spot desert bighorn sheep grazing there. A four-wheel-drive road, the
Shafer Trail, follows the White Rim all the way around the
Island in the Sky. Almost due east is Monument Basin,
with its white-capped red rock fins and spires. In the distance to the east (left) of the Colorado River is the Needles
District, where most of the park's long-distance wilder-

ness hiking trails are located. On the opposite side of the
Green River, to the southwest, is The Maze. The far rim of
The Maze is accessible only by an 80-mile four-wheel-
drive road; in The Maze itself there are no developed
trails. South as far as you can see, beyond the river junction, the Colorado disappears into Cataract Canyon,
which many river rafters and kayakers consider the ultimate challenge in North America. A member of John Wesley Powell's 1869 Colorado River exploration team
likened a boat trip down Cataract Canyon to riding "on
the back of the dragon." Beyond Cataract Canyon is an
area known simply as Ernie's Country. No road goes
there.

There are few developed trails in this district of
Canyonlands. The best hiking is in the area of Upheaval
Dome, the crater of a collapsed salt dome. Two easy trails,
each a one-mile, half-hour walk, leave from the Dome
Road near the picnic area. Upheaval Dome Trail goes to
the rim of the dome, with views into the center of the crater. Whale Rock Trail takes you to the top of a butte to
view the dome from a distance. You can enjoy a longer
hike along the Canyonlands rim from any of the overlooks, following the unofficial tracks of past hikers. Stay
on the bare slickrock surfaces, away from vegetation; that
way you won't disturb the fragile soil layer, and rattlesnakes won't disturb you.

Admission to all units of Canyonlands National Park,
good for 7 days, is $3 per vehicle.

Camping

The park's primitive 13-site campground is near Green
River Overlook, 7 miles in from the visitors center. There
are rest rooms but no water. Camping is free. The campground may be full by 6:00 p.m., or earlier in spring and
fall.

If the campground at Island in the Sky is full when you
arrive, go back outside the park boundary to the 7-mile
paved side road to **Dead Horse Point State Park**,
where you'll find a campground with all facilities and

well-developed rim trails overlooking the Colorado River
Canyon. Camping costs $9 (including the $3 entrance
fee), so this campground fills up less often than the free
one in Canyonlands. Another alternative is to spend the
night at **Arches National Park** (see Day 11) and hike the
Devil's Garden in the hours before dark or after dawn.

Lodging

Moab has a good selection of moderately priced accommodations. Chain motels includes the **Best Western
Green Well Motel**, 105 S. Main, (801) 259-6151, $79 in
summer (as low as $34 off-season); the **Ramada Inn**, 182
S. Main, (801) 259-7141, $79 in summer (as low as $34 off-
season); and the **Travelodge**, 550 S. Main, (801) 259-6171,
$64 ($50 off-season). Independent motels charge less.
The **Kokopelli Lodge**, 72 S. First East, (801) 259-7615,
offers newly remodeled rooms for about $45. For budget
accommodations, try the **Inca Inn Motel**, 570 N. Main,
(801) 259-2761, with rooms starting at $33 in the summer,
$23 off-season, or the **Red Rock Motel**, 51 N. 100 St.
West, (801) 259-5431, $40.

Moab's bed and breakfasts are small, so reservations
should be made in advance. **Cedar Breaks Condos**,
Center and Fourth East, (801) 259-7830, offers deluxe
lodging in individual condos with kitchens, living rooms,
and separate bedrooms, full breakfast included, for $60
double. The **Westwood Guest House**, 81 E. First South,
(801)-259-7283, has three-room suites with kitchens and
queen-size beds for under $60 a night.

Low-budget accommodations can be found at the
Lazy Lizard, an independent hostel located one mile
south of town behind A-1 Storage. Double rooms cost
$17.00. Facilities include a kitchen, laundry room, and
hot tub. Phone (801) 259-6057.

Food

Moab is the place to stock up on groceries. There are
three downtown supermarkets; you won't see another
one until you reach Kanab, Utah, three days from now.

Sixteen kinds of sandwiches, daily lunch and dinner specials, and breakfast anytime are served at **The Westerner**, 331 N. Main. This self-proclaimed historic landmark diner dates back to the 1950s uranium boom, when the original section was a "Wichita special"—a trailer towed to Moab to feed hordes of hungry prospectors.

The **Bar M Chuckwagon Supper** operates from June through September. Located on the bank of Mill Creek, on the south edge of town off 400 East Street, this ranch-style open-air restarant serves barbecued beef chuckwagon style, followed by real cowboys singing old-timey cowboy songs just like in a Roy Rogers movie. Call 259-2276 for dinner and show times.

Honest Ozzie's Cafe, 60 N. 100 West Street, 259-8442, serves the best vegetarian food in southern Utah as well as tempting all-natural, not-quite-vegetarian dishes.

The **Grand Old Ranch House**, 1266 Highway 191 N, 259-5753, serves dinner only (5:00-10:30 p.m. daily) in a turn-of-the-century farmhouse on the National Register of Historic Places. German cuisine is a specialty.

Itinerary Option

The Moab area has become a mountain bikers' mecca. In the spring and fall months, off-road cycling enthusiasts come by the thousands to ride in and around Canyonlands. Tour companies including **Rim Tours** (94 W. 100 North Street, 259-5223), **Kaibab Mountain Bike Tours** (37 S. 100 West Street, 259-7423), **Western Spirit Cycling** (545 Locust Lane, 259-8723), and **Adrift Adventures** (378 N. Main, 259-8594) offer guided tours of the canyon country. Day trips cost $40 to $50 per person, and four-day trips into the heart of Canyonlands cost $320 to $400 per person. Kaibab Mountain Bike Tours offers a combination biking, hiking, and rafting trip to Cataract Canyon for around $700. All of these tour outfitters also rent out mountain bikes for individual riding at around $25 a day. Without a tour, you can ride the **Moab Slickrock Bike Trail**, which starts about 2 miles out of town on Sand Flats Road past the city dump. The challenging 10-mile loop trail crosses spectacular undulating expanses of bare rock as it follows an often-steep, winding, sometimes edgy route originally established by off-road motorcyclists but now taken over by bicycles. The trail passes magnificent viewpoints along Negro Bill Canyon and Swiss Cheese Ridge.

ARCHES TO CAPITOL REEF

Today holds what may be a once-in-a-lifetime experience: three national parks in the same day. Awaken in Canyonlands and get an early start to tour Arches. Drive during the middle of the day, with a possible stop at Goblin Valley if the weather isn't too hot, and arrive at Capitol Reef in time to enjoy the cool of the evening in the least known of Utah's national parks.

Suggested Schedule	
7:30 a.m.	Drive to Arches National Park.
8:00 a.m.	See Arches, hike.
12:00 noon	Drive to Green River.
1:30 p.m.	Drive to Goblin Valley.
2:30 p.m.	See Goblin Valley.
3:30 p.m.	Drive to Capitol Reef. Camp there or spend the night in nearby Torrey, Bicknell, or Loa.

Arches National Park

Arches is almost adjacent to Canyonlands. To get there, retrace your route from Island in the Sky to US 191 and go 6 miles east (back toward Moab) to the Arches National Park entrance. Park admission is $3 per vehicle.

Readers of *Desert Solitaire*, the late Edward Abbey's memoir of a season as a ranger in the small, almost inaccessible Arches National Monument in the 1950s, will recall his tirade against "national parkification" and, understandably, brace themselves for a bad case of too many tourists. In reality, it's not that bad. There is traffic on the park's paved roads, and the park service has put up signs telling you the names of all the major rock formations, but it's hardly Disneyland. Arrive as early in the morning as possible to beat both the heat and the press of other tourists.

Arches National Park, more than half of which is bare rock, centers around a collapsed salt dome similar to

Canyonlands' Upheaval Dome but larger. Salt deposits from ancient seas floated up to form a large underground deposit that fractured surface layers of sandstone, then groundwater dissolved the salt and washed it away. The dome collapsed, leaving a rim of fin formations, which freezing and thawing carved to make natural arches. The park has more natural arches than any other place in the world.

You can't appreciate Arches from behind a steering wheel. In fact, you can drive every road in the park and never understand its attraction. This is hiking country, with ten outstanding trails. The hike that will show you the most in a half-day visit is the Devil's Garden Trail from the campground at the end of the 21-mile main road. This moderate 5-mile loop trail leads to seven arches, including Landscape Arch, the world's longest natural span. It is the most popular trail in the park. For more remote hiking, turn off the main road on the unpaved road to Wolfe Ranch. At the old ranch cabin, you'll find the trailhead for Delicate Arch Trail, a steep 3-mile round-trip to perhaps the park's most beautiful arch. Allow three to four hours for either hike.

Travel Route: Arches to Capitol Reef (171 miles)

From the Arches National Park entrance, turn right (northwest) on US 191 and go 26 miles to Crescent Junction. Take I-70 westbound for 20 miles to Green River. Green River State Park, on the outskirts of town, has expansive green lawns and shade trees, a cool and pleasant picnic spot that could be worth the $3/day use fee.

Eleven miles west of Green River, exit the interstate southbound on UT Highway 24 to Hanksville, a distance of 51 miles. At 30 miles, you'll see a large sign on the right to Goblin Valley State Park. If you have time, take the 11-mile (last 6 unpaved) road into the park. There is a $2/day use fee. Goblin Valley's weird rock formations are unlike any other weird rock formations you've seen: imagine giant petrified milk chocolate-covered Walt Disney mushrooms, set against a backdrop of buttes eroded to resemble Mayan pyramids. If you can imagine that,

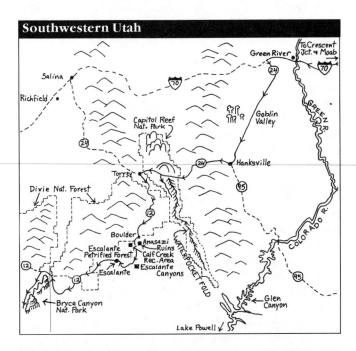

Southwestern Utah

you'll love this place. It may be too hot to walk through the valley in midafternoon. If you'd like to spend the night here and see it in the early evening but don't want to pay the $8 camping fee (there's no water anyway), camp free around the other side of the butte on the Wild Horse Butte road, which branches off just before the park entrance.

From Hanksville, continuing on UT 24, it's 30 miles to the entrance of Capitol Reef National Park.

Capitol Reef National Park

Capitol Reef may be the national park system's best-kept secret. Established in 1971, it remains the least visited of Utah's national parks. Besides offering a variety of short and long hiking trails, unpaved auto roads, four-wheel-drive roads, and trackless wilderness, the park protects ancient petroglyphs, a well-preserved Mormon pioneer village, and orchards where visitors can pick fruit right off the trees. Admission to the park is $3 per vehicle.

The park's most visible points of interest, listed in order below, cluster along UT 24 on the 9-mile drive up the Fremont River from the entrance gate to the visitors center and campground. Take your time. Tomorrow morning you'll have a chance to sample the park's backcountry.

Sightseeing Highlights

▲ **Behunin Cabin**—Elijah Behunin, the area's first settler (1882), lived with his wife and ten children in this stone cabin, which was smaller than most modern camping vehicles. The next time you have to huddle in your rig or tent until the rain stops, think of Elijah.

▲ **Hickman Bridge**—A one-mile (each way) trail climbs switchbacks 380 feet through a small canyon and under the 133-foot natural bridge. Along the way are Indian ruins and fine views of white-capped domes, including Capitol Dome, for which the "reef" (uplifted cliff) is named. Allow two hours for the hike.

▲▲ **Petroglyphs**—Fremont Indians, who lived here at least as early as A.D. 800, left this rock art for us to admire. Experts do not know its meaning; do you? The best petroglyphs are reached on a short, easy trail from the parking pullout.

▲ **Fruita Schoolhouse**—This country school served the pioneer community of Fruita (originally named "The Eden of Wayne County"), where the visitors center and campground are now located. The school, used from 1896 to 1941, is the only building left standing.

▲▲ **Orchards**—While no houses remain from old Fruita, the 2,500 cherry, apple, peach, and apricot trees that were the village's lifeblood endure, preserved by the National Park Service as a Historic Landscape. Pruning, irrigation, and replanting are done by park service employees. When the fruit ripens, the public is invited to pick it, then pay the park service the same price per pound that local orchards get. Harvest dates are posted at the visitors center.

▲▲ **Fremont River Trail**—An easy walk upriver from the campground through the orchards will bring you to the trail, which follows the riverbank for half a mile. If you're feeling adventurous and have at least 2½ hours, stay on the trail for the steep climb—800 feet in three-quarters of a mile—up Miner's Peak for a fine view of Fruita and the reef.

▲▲ **Cohab Canyon Trail**—Starting just across the road from the campground, this trail climbs a quarter-mile by switchbacks to a slickrock canyon, goes almost 2 miles through the canyon, and comes out at the river across the road from the Hickman Bridge trailhead. (Cohab Canyon and Hickman Bridge trails can be combined for a great all-morning hike.) The canyon got its name because, so the story goes, Mormon "cohabitationists" used it to hide out from U.S. marshals trying to enforce the federal law against polygamy.

Camping

Fruita Campground at Capitol Reef National Park is the only federal campground in the Southwest with a green lawn at each campsite. It is on the riverbank, surrounded by orchards, with two trails (described above) for evening or morning walks; $5 per night. Nightly naturalist slide shows are presented at the campground amphitheater from May through September.

If you're traveling in July or August, and you arrive after 6:00 p.m., you may find the Capitol Reef campground full. There are three national forest campgrounds higher in the mountains, within 20 miles southeast of Torrey on UT 12. The first, **Singletree**, offers a good view of the valley and beyond to the Henry Mountains, the last place in the lower 48 United States to be explored and mapped. **Pleasant Creek** and neighboring **Oak Creek** campgrounds are said to have marauding skunks ("*Thousands* of skunks!" according to the campground host). Stash all food inside your vehicle at night.

Lodging

This national park has no lodge. You'll find a few motels, as well as restaurants and service stations, in the towns of Torrey (11 miles from the visitors center on US 24), Bicknell (19 miles), and Loa (26 miles).

CAPITOL REEF TO BRYCE CANYON

The drive from Capitol Reef to Bryce Canyon, by way of
Escalante Canyons, is among the most beautiful stretches
of road on this tour. Bryce Canyon is congested with
tourist traffic, but the scenery is worth braving the masses
for. Test your crowd-avoiding strategy (which will also
work at the Grand Canyon) by taking an easy walk along
the canyon rim or a more demanding one down among
the hoodoos.

Suggested Schedule

9:00 a.m.	Capitol Reef Scenic Drive and/or hike.
12:00 noon	Drive to Escalante Canyons.
1:00 p.m.	Picnic.
2:00 p.m.	Drive to Bryce Canyon.
3:00 p.m.	Get campsite (or check into lodge).
3:30 p.m.	See Bryce Canyon National Park.

Capitol Reef Scenic Drive

Spend the morning hiking in Capitol Reef or take the
8-mile unpaved Scenic Drive south from the visitors center. Take time to look at the gigantic 3-D relief map in the
visitors center first. A self-guided tour brochure, available
free at the visitors center, explains the area's geology.

The last 2 miles of the Scenic Drive were once (from
1884 to 1962) part of the main "highway" through south-
central Utah. Beyond the end of the Scenic Drive, the old
road continues as Capitol Gorge Trail. An easy 2-mile
round-trip hike takes you to Indian petroglyphs, a pioneer register, and The Tanks—pockets in the rock which
capture rainwater pools, hence the other name for the
Capitol Reef formation, Waterpocket Fold. Butch Cassidy,
for years a hero in these parts as he robbed from the rich
(plundering trains and banks all over the Four Corners
region) and shared with the poor (including not only his
gang members but also local folks who guarded the

secret of his whereabouts), frequently used this route to reach his hideout nearby.

The scenic drive is not a loop. Drive back to the visitors center the same way you came.

Travel Route: Capitol Reef to Bryce Canyon (104 miles)

Drive west from Capitol Reef on UT 24 for 11 miles. As you near the town of Torrey, turn left (south) on UT 12 and stay on that highway all the way to Bryce Canyon National Park. The first 33 miles of the route climb into Dixie National Forest, through ponderosa forest between Boulder Mountain and Impossible Peak, and descend into the town of Boulder, where Anasazi Indian Village State Park is located.

From there, the highway descends into Escalante Canyons, a Bureau of Land Management Scenic Area. If the U.S. government ever decides southern Utah needs a sixth national park, this area and the adjoining Box-Death Hollow Wilderness will be the prime candidate. Until then, it's our secret. The best picnic stop-and-walk is Calf Creek Recreation Area, on your right about a mile before the bottom of the canyon, where a 2-mile trail leads past two Anasazi village ruins to Calf Creek Falls. Beyond the canyons, 18 miles from Boulder, is the town of Escalante. The local attraction is Escalante Petrified Forest State Park ($3 entrance fee), which also has cliff dwellings. Forty-two more miles across grazing land will bring you to the entrance of Bryce Canyon National Park. Admission to the national park is $5 per vehicle.

Bryce Canyon National Park

Brace yourself for Bryce Canyon, a victim of its own success. Anytime between Memorial Day and Labor Day, it will be crowded. Bryce Canyon (formerly Utah National Monument) became a national park in 1923, just four years after the Grand Canyon did. Its proximity to the Grand Canyon makes it an ideal stop on loop tours that take in the North Rim, Zion, and Glen Canyon Dam.

Many times more tourists visit Bryce Canyon than Island in the Sky, Arches, and Capitol Reef combined. The 18-mile paved drive through the park has traffic at all times, and the scenic overlook pullouts are about as much fun as a shopping mall parking lot.

Fortunately, there's a way to beat the crowds at Bryce: walk. Few visitors do, though the park has 60 miles of beautifully maintained trails. I suggest you skip the drive to the far end of the park. The most spectacular formations can be seen on the easy Rim Trail that runs 6 miles from Fairyland View to Sunset Point, Sunrise Point, and finally Bryce Point. Take part or all of it. A shuttle service is available for one-way hikes. More ambitious hikers with at least five hours to spend can get down among the hoodoos on the strenuous 5½-mile Fairyland Loop Trail, which also runs between Sunrise Point and Fairyland View, then take the shuttle back or walk back along the Rim Trail for a good view of where they've been.

The eroded shale-and-sandstone uplifts of Bryce Canyon are absolutely unique. The park service even invented a new name for the white and bright orange obelisks and spires: "hoodoo," which they define as "a pinnacle, pillar, or odd-shaped rock left standing by the forces of erosion." Bryce Canyon, by the way, was named after Ebenezer Bryce, a homesteader who tried to graze cattle here between 1875 and 1880. Bryce's opinion of the scenery was, "It's a hell of a place to lose a cow."

Camping
Bryce Canyon has two campgrounds, **North Campground** and **Sunset Campground**. Together they have 218 campsites, with separate loops for RVs and tent campers. By around 5:00 p.m., the campsite registration areas will be a traffic jam of campers and motor homes. Stake your claim to a campsite as soon as you arrive in the park and sightsee afterward. Both campgrounds have campfire programs. Campsites cost $7 to $11. Pay showers and laundry facilities, as well as pay telephones, are available at the Sunrise Point Camper Store.

Lodging

For a roof over your head, you can do no better than a room or cabin at **Bryce Canyon Lodge**, (801) 834-7686, in the park. The rustic elegance is a bargain at $63 to $74 a night. Reservations are a must. Main lodge units have two queen-size beds, full bath, and private porch. The carpeted cabins have fireplaces.

Other accommodations near the park entrance include **Best Western Ruby's Inn**, (801) 834-7686, $68 in season (as low as $34 in winter); and **Bryce Canyon Pines**, (801) 834-5336, $60 in season ($40 off-season).

Food

Fine dining can be found at the **Bryce Canyon Lodge** dining room. Groceries are sold at the **Camper Store** nearby.

GLEN CANYON DAM AND LEE'S FERRY

After a leisurely, slow-to-get-going morning at Bryce
Canyon, drive down to the Colorado River. You saw it on
Day 10 from Island in the Sky, and you'll see it again
tomorrow from the rim of the Grand Canyon. Today,
you'll see the river in two of its other aspects: from the
top of its largest dam and, just a few miles downriver,
from the exact spot where the Grand Canyon begins.

Suggested Schedule

9:00 a.m.	Take a hike at Bryce Canyon.
11:00 a.m.	Drive from Bryce Canyon to Kanab. Lunch there.
1:30 p.m.	Drive to Glen Canyon Dam.
3:00 p.m.	Take the dam tour.
4:30 p.m.	Drive to Lee's Ferry.
5:30 p.m.	Camp at Lee's Ferry.

Travel Route: Bryce Canyon to Lee's Ferry (126 miles)

Leaving Bryce Canyon, take UT 12 westbound, 13 miles
through Red Canyon to the intersection with US 89. From
here on, it's impossible to get lost. Just follow the big
green-and-white "Grand Canyon" signs. Turn south (left)
on US 89 and stay on it all the way to Kanab, 61 miles.
Along the way, watch on your left for the privately operated Moqui Cave. If you like caves, here's one; but the real
attraction is the entrance in the shape of a triceratops—a
classic bit of tourist kitsch.

There's a supermarket in Kanab, in case you're low on
provisions by now. From Kanab, stay on US 89 to Lake
Powell. The driving distance to Glen Canyon Dam is 85
miles.

After touring the dam, continue south for 23 more
miles, across the corner of the Navajo Reservation, to Bit-
ter Springs, where Alternate US 89 turns north (right) to

Marble Canyon. Another 14 miles will bring you to Navajo Bridge, the first bridge across the Colorado River when it was built in the 1920s. Just past the village of Marble Canyon, follow the 4-mile road on your right (north) to Lee's Ferry, Glen Canyon National Recreation Area.

Sightseeing Highlights
▲▲ **Glen Canyon Dam**—The northernmost and largest of the dams that form the Colorado River Project (the other major ones are Hoover Dam on Lake Mead, Davis Dam on Lake Mojave, and Parker Dam on Lake Havasu), Glen Canyon Dam generates unimaginable amounts of electricity and sends it by power lines straight across 600 miles of desert to southern California. Take the guided tour into the bowels of the dam to see the water turbines and the long row of transformers, each of which pours out 345,000 volts of electricity.

Environmentalists have never forgiven the government for building this dam, which flooded one of the last unexplored areas in the United States. It may seem strange that, with all this water and energy, the surrounding land is arid and empty. Virtually none of the water in the Colorado River or its reservoirs is used for irrigation until it reaches southern California. About one-third of the river's water evaporates from the lake surfaces. What remains is diverted by pipeline just north of the Mexican border to irrigate the Imperial Valley. Glen Canyon Dam traps Colorado River silt, sand, and mining wastes, filling up the lakebed several feet each year. In less than two centuries, experts say, Lake Powell will be a vast barren mud flat, while the dam, its generators rusted and silent, will be one of the world's largest man-made waterfalls. (Powell Falls National Monument? Squint your eyes and you can almost see it.)

The visitors center is open daily from 7:00 a.m. to 7:00 p.m. during the summer months and 8:30 a.m. to 5:30 p.m. the rest of the year.

Change your watch when you cross the dam. Arizona does not change to daylight saving time, as other south-

western states do. Most Arizonans live in the hot climate
of Phoenix and Tucson, where they prefer long cool summer evenings, not more daylight. When it's 3:00 p.m. on
the Utah side of the dam, it's 4:00 p.m. on the Arizona
side.

▲ **John Wesley Powell Museum**—This free museum at
Lake Powell Boulevard and Navajo Drive in Page, about 2
miles past the dam on the Arizona side, recounts the
adventures of the man who led the first expedition down
the Colorado River through Cataract Canyon and the
Grand Canyon (1869), braving the white water in wooden
boats. There are also Indian artifacts and exhibits that
explain the geology of the river and its canyons. The
museum is open weekdays from 8:00 a.m. to 6:00 p.m.,
Tuesdays until 8:00 p.m., and Sundays from 10:00 a.m. to
6:00 p.m., closed Saturdays, during the summer months;
in the spring and October, it closes at 5:00 p.m. and is not
open on weekends; closed during the winter months.
Admission is free.

▲ **Lee's Ferry**—John D. Lee established the first ferry
across the Colorado River here in Marble Canyon in 1871.
He was a fugitive at the time for leading fellow Mormons
to massacre a wagon train of California-bound pioneers.
He came here to hide, went into business, and lived here
with one of his 17 wives until U.S. marshals found him
and shot him.

Lee's Ferry is still the only road to river level on the
Colorado between Green River, Utah, and the California
state line, a distance of over 600 river miles. Though just a
few miles downriver from Glen Canyon Dam, here in
Marble Canyon you'll find rare, wild beauty barely
touched by mankind. Lee's Ferry is the departure point
for all white-water rafting and kayaking expeditions into
the Grand Canyon. You can watch them set out any
morning from the launch ramp at the end of the road.

On the river, across the main road from the campground, is a long sandy beach, the easiest water access for
area wildlife and the only place you're likely to spot a
beaver in the desert. Temperatures by the river are much

cooler than at the campground. As you bask on the beach, notice the narrow strip of white limestone that rises diagonally out of the water on the cliffs across the river. Here is where the Grand Canyon begins: the white layer keeps slanting upward to become the surface of the Kaibab Plateau, the rim of the Grand Canyon.

Camping
Lee's Ferry Campground has rest rooms, water, and picnic tables with shade roofs. Used primarily by fishermen, the campground is crowded on weekends but practically empty during the week. There are no hookups. The camping fee is $6.

Lodging
Page (pop. 6,500), on the Arizona side of Glen Canyon Dam, has a handful of motor inns that cater primarily to boating enthusiasts, such as the **Holiday Inn/Lake Powell** (287 N. Lake Powell Boulevard, 602-645-8851, $82 to $92 double) and the **Inn at Lake Powell** (formerly a Ramada Inn, 716 Rim View Drive, 602-645-2466, $64 to $80 double, significantly less off-season).

Itinerary Option
For information on all-day boat excursions from Glen Canyon Dam to **Rainbow Bridge National Monument**, 50 miles northwest and only accessible by water, contact the Superintendent, Glen Canyon National Recreation Area, Box 1507, Page, AZ 86040, (602) 645-2471. To arrange boat rentals or charters and find out about privately operated tours, call Wahweap Marina, (602) 645-2433.

THE GRAND CANYON: NORTH RIM

The North Rim of the Grand Canyon is a thousand feet higher than the South Rim—8,255 feet above sea level and about 4,300 feet above the Colorado River in the bottom of the canyon. Some people contend that the view is better from the South Rim, because you can see the river from there. I like the North Rim view just fine, the climate is cooler, and this side of the canyon is less visited and less extensively developed.

Suggested Schedule

8:30 a.m.	Drive to Jacob Lake.
10:00 a.m.	Drive to Grand Canyon North Rim.
12:00 noon	Arrive at North Rim. Get a campsite or check into the lodge.
1:00 p.m.	Relax on a gentle walk along the Transept Trail to the lodge and out to Bright Angel Point.
Evening	Dine in or out. Catch the campfire talk or join a night sky walk to Bright Angel Point.

Travel Route: Lee's Ferry to Grand Canyon North Rim (83 miles)

Get an early start. The Grand Canyon North Rim campground sometimes fills up by noon.

A 41-mile drive west on US 89 Alternate will take you up through the ponderosa pine forests of the Kaibab Plateau to Jacob Lake. Turn south on AZ 67. Near the intersection, you'll see a park service portable building by the side of the road. Stop for information on campsite availability at the Grand Canyon. If there is any problem, the rangers will direct you to alternate campgrounds in the national forest.

From Jacob Lake, it's 42 more miles on AZ 67 to the North Rim. Admission to the Grand Canyon is $10 per

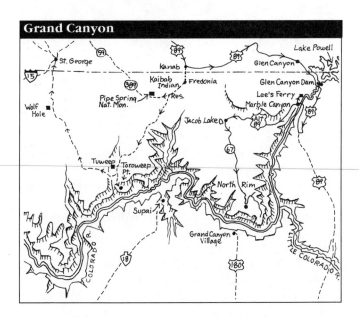

vehicle. Be sure to save your receipt; it is valid for 7 days and will also get you into the South Rim (Day 19).

The Grand Canyon

Even at the Grand Canyon, one of the nation's most popular parks, you can find solitude by hiking one of the trails that lead to more isolated points along the rim. Some are longer than others, but all are level and easy to walk.

The popular Transept Trail leads 1½ miles from the campground to the lodge along the canyon rim. An extension of the trail from the lodge goes another quarter-mile to Bright Angel Point. Take this walk as soon as you've arranged your campsite or lodging, and think, "Wow! The Grand Canyon!"

A longer and less-frequented route is the Uncle Jim Trail, which starts from the North Kaibab Trailhead. From the campground, cross the main road and follow the path around the water tanks; when you reach the road again, you're there. Follow the trail that goes back into the woods, not the one that goes down into the canyon. It is a 5-mile round-trip walk to Uncle Jim Point (named for Jim Owens, the warden of Grand Canyon Game Preserve until it became a national park in 1919). Allow three hours for the walk.

The Ken Patrick Trail branches to the left from Uncle Jim Trail 1 mile along and goes another 10 miles (one way) to Point Imperial. The hike takes six hours each way. It goes deep into the forest but only affords canyon views around Point Imperial, to which you can also drive. The most practical plan for hiking this trail is to drive to Point Imperial and walk partway back along the trail, or arrange for someone less athletic than you to drive out there in six hours and pick you up.

Perhaps the most enjoyable rim walk in the park is the Widforss Trail. The trailhead is 1 mile in on a dirt road that leaves the main road 1¼ miles from the campground, one-quarter mile from the Cape Royal Road junction. This 10-mile round-trip (allow five hours) skirts the Transept rim, then takes you into the forest and brings you back to the rim overlooking Haunted Canyon. There is a picnic area at Widforss Point (named for Gunnar Widforss, a Swedish artist who made a career of painting America's national parks in the 1920s).

I wrote in earlier editions of this book, "It is not possible to hike to the bottom of the Grand Canyon and back the same day." But travel agent Betty Schmitt of St. Louis, Missouri, recently informed me that it *is* possible. At age 52, with her 13-year-old daughter, Betty, she did hike from the North Rim to the river and back—starting long before dawn, reaching the bottom at 7:00 a.m., and getting back after dark. The 27-mile trip took 18 hours of hiking. I'm impressed!

You can hike partway down the North Kaibab Trail, but be warned: the first part of the trail is the steepest, dropping 2,000 feet in not much more than a mile. Climbing back up will take four times as long as going down. An all-day, 9½-mile round-trip hike to the swimming holes near where Roaring Springs Canyon joins

Bright Angel Creek will make you feel like you've hiked the Grand Canyon.

Camping
North Rim Campground, perched practically on the edge of the Grand Canyon, has 86 campsites, first-come, first-served. The campground has a laundromat and coin-operated showers. This is not a large campground for such a popular area. In fact, the North Rim has only about one-third the campground capacity of Bryce Canyon. If the campground is full, as it may well be if you arrive later than noon, the rangers at the Jacob Lake information booth will point you toward another campground in the national forest and tell you what time to line up if you want a North Rim campsite tomorrow. To assure a campsite at the rim, you can make reservations (at least a month in advance) by mail through TICKETRON Reservation Office, P.O. Box 617516, Chicago, IL 60661-7516, or by calling (800) 452-1111 with your Visa or MasterCard in hand. Camping fees start at $10.

Lodging
Grand Canyon Lodge, the only North Rim accommodation within the park, offers modern guest rooms as well as three types of individual cabins. Prices range between $46 and $63 double. Make reservations well in advance by calling 638-2611.

Slightly lower-cost accommodations, with a pleasant forest setting but no canyon view, can be found at **Jacob Lake Inn**, (602) 643-7232. Rates range from $48 to $56, with cottages for $62.

Food
The dining room at the **Grand Canyon Lodge**, with its panoramic picture window view, serves a limited selection of fine food at moderate prices, breakfast, lunch, and dinner. Reservations are essential for dinner; go to the lodge and make them in person. Breakfast overlooking the Grand Canyon is an experience to remember.

Itinerary Option: Toroweap Point
If solitude is what you crave and a 140-mile drive on
unpaved roads doesn't intimidate you, allow an extra day
in your itinerary for a drive out to Toroweap Point at the
west end of the canyon, where you can be alone on the
rim for a more personal Grand Canyon experience.

This route involves driving on unpaved roads for 67
miles to Toroweap Point today and another 67 (or more)
unpaved miles back out tomorrow. The roads are wide
and well graded—better, in fact, than some paved highways you've driven on the Navajo Reservation—but there
is no gas, food, or water anywhere. Nobody lives out
here. If your vehicle breaks down and you can't fix it, you
may have a long wait before anyone comes along and can
fetch help, so carry twice as much food and water as you
think you'll need. Don't try this trip if thunderstorms
threaten: flash floods are possible, and the road can be
slippery when wet. Storms occur in the afternoon,
almost never in the morning, so if you can get there, you
can count on being able to get back.

From the North Rim, retrace your route to Jacob Lake
and Fredonia, a distance of 75 miles. At Fredonia, turn
west (left) on AZ 389 and go 15 miles to **Pipe Springs
National Monument** on the Kaibab Paiute Indian Reservation. Around the 9-mile point on the way, watch for the
unpaved road that goes south. This is the road you'll
want to take after seeing Pipe Springs.

A well-preserved remnant of Mormon pioneer life, the
ranch that is now Pipe Springs National Monument was
established to graze cattle tithed to the church by ranchers
throughout the Arizona Strip. The founder's name was
Winsor so, naturally enough, the fortresslike stone main
house bears the nickname, "Winsor Castle." As the only
telegraph station in the Strip, the ranch became a commu-
nications center. Women from the historical society in
Fredonia, wearing authentic period dress, demonstrate
weaving, quilting, and other pioneer crafts in the castle's
antique-furnished rooms. Open 8:00 a.m. to 5:00 p.m.

The drive to Toroweap Point takes you across the **Ari-**

zona Strip (no relation to the Las Vegas Strip). Pioneer ranchers discovered the area in the 1870s, at a time when there were several years of exceptional rainfall. Thinking they'd discovered a cattleman's paradise, they moved large beef herds into the area. Then the rain stopped. The cattle overgrazed the sparse vegetation, then starved. Today a handful of Paiute and Anglo ranchers run a few cattle over the vast area, but you're more likely to see pronghorn antelope.

The signs on the road to Toroweap are confusing. The inconspicuous sign at the highway turnoff says the road goes to Mt. Trumbull. Follow signs to "Tuweap," "Toroweap," or "Grand Canyon National Monument" whenever you see them, but pay no attention to the distances posted, which are wildly contradictory. Otherwise, just stay on what looks like the most-used road at each fork and maintain a southerly direction. A three-hour drive (60 miles) across the Arizona Strip will bring you to the Grand Canyon National Park boundary fence. There is a house near the entrance where a park ranger used to live, but it apparently hasn't been occupied in some time. The last 7 miles to the rim are bumpier. The informal campground is all the way at the end of the road, on the very tip of Toroweap Point.

Toroweap Point is the Grand Canyon's "back door," a wilderness area that hardly anyone sees. The last time I was there, on a Saturday afternoon in the middle of the tourist season, the only other visitors were a painter and a photographer. On weekdays you may find yourself completely alone on the canyon rim.

The rim here is lower than in the main part of the park. The approach to Toroweap Point is through a notch in the upper rim, so the point is actually on the hot, dry slickrock inner rim, the one you overlook from the North Rim, and about 100 miles downriver. The Colorado River is nearly 2,000 feet below you, between sheer cliffs. You can watch tiny-looking river rafts as they float past. The silence and the canyon's acoustics actually make it possible to eavesdrop on rafters' conversations. Toroweap

Point also affords the only view of a major Grand Canyon formation, Vulcan's Throne.

When you leave Toroweap Point, instead of backtracking to rejoin the main itinerary at Fredonia, you can take a different unpaved road across the Arizona Strip to rejoin the main 22-day itinerary at St. George. The shortcut is 97 miles, all unpaved road, compared to 67 miles of unpaved road and 90 miles of highway. If you take the shortcut, you'll miss Zion National Park and save as much as an hour of driving time, depending on road conditions. To take this shortcut, backtrack 14 miles north from Toroweap Point, then take the road that forks to the left (west) to Mt. Trumbull. Twenty miles on, the road turns north. Stay on the same lonely road north for 63 more miles, and you'll suddenly come to St. George and I-15. Allow four to five hours for the drive.

ZION AND VALLEY OF FIRE

You can't cross the Grand Canyon by road. To get to the other side of the Colorado River, drive west beyond the end of the canyon, past Lake Mead, and across Hoover Dam. This route will bring you within a stone's throw of Las Vegas. Take time along the way to see Zion National Park and enjoy a warm desert night at the Valley of Fire, then enter the city tomorrow morning.

Suggested Schedule	
8:30 a.m.	Breakfast at North Rim Lodge.
10:00 a.m.	Drive to Kanab.
12:00 noon	Drive to Zion National Park.
1:00 p.m.	Explore Zion.
3:30 p.m. or later	Zion to I-15 to Valley of Fire.
Evening	Camp at Valley of Fire, or stay in Las Vegas.

Travel Route: Grand Canyon via Zion to Valley of Fire (256 miles)

From the Grand Canyon North Rim, retrace your Day 14 route 75 miles north to Fredonia (where people returning from Toroweap Point rejoin the main route). Stay on US 89 for 17 more miles until you come to Mount Carmel Junction, then turn left on UT 9 to Zion National Park. Pay the $5 per vehicle fee. (Note for motor-homers: Any vehicle wider than 7'10" or higher than 11'4" must be escorted through the tunnel. There is a $10 fee for this.)

From the entrance to Zion, it's 51 miles westbound on UT 9, through the town of Hurricane, to St. George, southwestern Utah's largest city (pop. 12,000), where you will join I-15 southbound. A long, scenic descent through the Virgin River Gorge will drop you into the Mojave Desert, the lowest elevation and hottest place on this tour route. Thirteen miles south on the interstate, you will cross into Arizona briefly; 26 more miles will bring

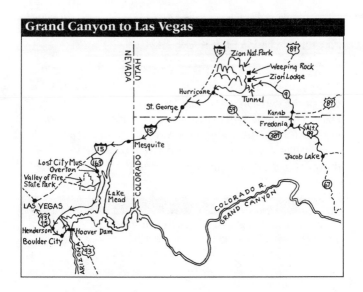

Grand Canyon to Las Vegas

you to the Nevada state line. Thirty miles into Nevada, at the Glendale exit, leave I-15, follow NV 169 nine miles past the town of Overton and take the road that turns right (west) to Valley of Fire State Park.

If you'd like to get in out of the heat for a while, visit Lost City Museum in Overton, a comprehensive exhibit of the early Pueblo culture that thrived here around A.D. 800. Open daily from 8:30 a.m. to 4:30 p.m. Admission is $1 per adult, free for those under age 18.

If you can't wait to get your hand on a slot machine handle or your head under a roof (air-conditioned), simply stay on I-15 for one more hour and you'll find yourself in the middle of Las Vegas. Hop off the interstate at Sahara Boulevard and go east a few blocks to Las Vegas Boulevard South, better known as the Strip.

Sightseeing Highlights

▲▲ **Zion National Park**—When early Mormon settler Isaac Behunin named this spectacular stretch of gorge Little Zion after the heavenly city of God, he was quite serious. "These great mountains," he declared, "are natural temples of God. We can worship here as well as in the man-made temples." Zion became a national park in 1918, a year before the Grand Canyon did.

Zion is the quintessential scenic drive, a brief but intense burst of visual glory midway between the Grand Canyon and Las Vegas. The main road, with its long tunnel, tantalizing peek-aboo windows, and sudden descent into Zion Canyon, is worth the price of admission.

But people who don't get out of their cars can only catch a too-brief glimpse of Zion's beauty. Start with the short, easy walk to Weeping Rock from the parking area just past the main lodge.

You have time to explore. It's only two hours from here to your campground for the night, and if you arrive too early, it will still be very hot. Though most Zion back-country can only be reached on overnight hikes, any of the following trails makes a reasonable half-day or less hike: the Emerald Pools Trail starting at Zion Lodge, 1.2 miles round-trip; the Hidden Canyon Trail starting from the Weeping Rock parking area, 2 miles round-trip; the Gateway to the Narrows Trail starting at the Temple of Sinawava, 2 miles round-trip; the Canyon Overlook Trail starting from the tunnel overlook parking area, 1 mile, steep; or the Watchman Viewpoint Trail starting at the south campground, 2 miles round-trip, steep. Carry plenty of water!

▲▲ **Valley of Fire State Park**—White and red sandstone layers have fractured and eroded into a bewildering maze, best appreciated on a short hike into Mouse's Tank, where an Indian renegade named Old Mouse and about 50 followers hid out while raiding area ranches. It took the cavalry 11 years to find them. Thousand-year-old petroglyphs, scratched with wooden atlatls (spear-throwing sticks) in the soft stone surfaces by nomadic Indian hunters, decorate the walls of several canyons within the park. Hiking is best soon after dawn, when tracks of nighttime wildlife are fresh and the large white nocturnal flowers of the sacred datura are still open. You might even catch a rare glimpse of a desert bighorn sheep. Park admission is free.

Camping

Valley of Fire State Park Campground has 38 campsites, picnic tables, and running water. Staying here ena-
bles you to explore the park early in the morning.

South along Lake Mead Drive, you'll find lakeside
camping at **Overton Beach, Echo Bay**, and **Hemenway Beach**.

Lodging

Las Vegas is full of hotels. See the listings in Day 16.

Food

Buy any groceries you need in St. George. There is no
food service at or near the Valley of Fire. See tomorrow's
listings for dining in Las Vegas.

LAKE MEAD AND LAS VEGAS

Of all the subcultures that thrive in southwestern isolation—New Mexico's Norteños, the Mormons, and the various Native American groups—the newest and fastest growing is to be found in Las Vegas.

On this tour, you've seen example after dramatic example of nature in action. The nature you'll see in Las Vegas is human nature, the action takes seconds instead of centuries, and the wildlife feeds on casino chips. Think of it as Greed National Park and plunge deep into the air-conditioned fast-money clatter. But first, check out the countryside. While Las Vegas welcomes 13 million visitors each year, remarkably few leave the Strip or Glitter Gulch to see the varied and starkly beautiful landscapes that lie just outside of the city. Take time to drive the scenic route along the Lake Mead shore to Hoover Dam.

Suggested Schedule

8:00 a.m.	Explore Valley of Fire.
10:00 a.m.	Lake Mead drive.
12:30 p.m.	Hoover Dam to Las Vegas.
1:00 p.m.	Check into a casino hotel along the Strip.
1:30 p.m.	Clean up and cool off.
2:00 p.m.	Wander your hotel and those nearby, or visit a museum.
4:00 p.m.	Nap.
6:00 p.m.	Dinner.
Evening	Strip nightlife—stay out late.

Lake Mead Scenic Drive

After exploring the Valley of Fire early in the morning, exit the same way you came in. (If you continued in the same direction, out the park's other entrance, you'd come out on I-15, 33 miles north of the city.) Where the park road intersects the Lake Mead Scenic Drive, turn left (or continue straight for a brief stop at Overton Beach, 2 miles farther on, then return to the Lake Mead road).

Las Vegas/Lake Mead Area

The Lake Mead Scenic Drive parallels the shoreline for 42 miles, but for the first hour of the drive you won't see the lake from the road; instead, you'll follow dry Las Vegas Wash. Stop and let tiny tropical fish nibble your toes in Rogers Warm Spring, on your right. For a lake view, visit Echo Bay, two miles down a road on your left.

You know you're nearing the end of the Lake Mead road when you see often-lively Hemenway Beach and its campground. Stop and splash. The water's fine, though you'll want sandals because the beach is rocky. Warm and cold convection currents in the lake water tingle swimmers' skin. Use caution when wading: this is the rim of a flooded canyon, and not far from shore, submerged cliffs drop off into water 400 feet deep.

A few miles south of the beach, the road joins US 93. Turn left (east) and descend by switchbacks to Hoover Dam, the oldest dam on the Colorado River, completed in 1935. Tours ($1 per person) take you by elevator down through the center of the dam to the power plant, daily from 8:00 a.m. to 5:45 p.m. Memorial Day to Labor Day, 9:00 a.m. to 4:15 p.m. the rest of the year. See the large relief map of the Colorado River in the visitors center. Check out the dam's unusual art deco ornamentation, including winged sculptures called Figures of the Republic and a terrazzo representation of the solar system with astrological overtones.

Hoover Dam is also an impressive sight at night under lights. After dark, looking over the wall by the parking area on the Nevada side, you may see ringtail cats that inhabit the cliff, small elusive nocturnal desert cousins of the raccoon.

Leaving Hoover Dam the same way you came, stay on US 93 through Boulder City, which was the largest town in southern Nevada before World War II, and continue 23 miles to Las Vegas. US 93 is the city's eastern edge. To reach the Strip, turn left on Tropicana Road or Desert Inn Road. You can't miss it.

Las Vegas

Mormon pioneers tried to establish a fort settlement at Las Vegas ("The Meadows," named by a Mexican trading expedition scout) but failed. By 1864, when Nevada became a state, the area had no population at all. In 1931, when Nevada legalized gambling, Las Vegas was a small railroad and ranching town, seven blocks long, with a countywide population of 5,000.

El Rancho, the first casino resort on what is now the Strip, opened in 1941, but only after World War II, when Los Angeles (at a distance of 300 miles, the nearest city to Las Vegas) boomed, did casino development begin in earnest. In 1946, "Bugsy" Siegel built the lavish Flamingo, reputedly with organized crime backing. The rumor seemed to be confirmed when, six months later, Siegel was shot and killed by hit men in his Hollywood home. The Flamingo is now owned by the Hilton chain. Despite Las Vegas' gangster mystique, however, most casinos have never had any organized crime connections.

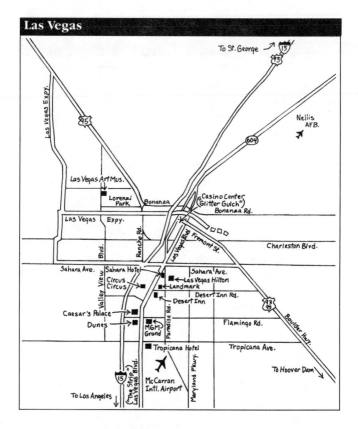

Today, Las Vegas has a population of over 600,000 —
more than half the population of the entire state of
Nevada.

On payday in the Old West, cowboys would head for
the nearest saloon town to drink, gamble, and chase
fancy women. Las Vegas serves the same purpose as those
old-time saloon towns but on a grand scale. Today's
casinos play host to cowboys and oil riggers from all over
the West as well as to millions of visitors who are neither.
Old-timers, who are often heard to refer to the city as
"Lost Wages," like to point out that "Vegas is where
Americans come to do all the things they could do at
home if they weren't so respectable."

To the north of Las Vegas is the U.S. Nuclear Testing
Site. The first nuclear weapon atmospheric tests were
conducted here in 1951, and each test became a local
event as picnickers gathered to see the mushroom cloud
75 miles away. Six years later, the nuclear tests were
moved underground, much to the disappointment of
spectators.

Las Vegas's major sightseeing highlights are the casino
hotels themselves. If gambling isn't your idea of fun, wander the maze of casinos anyway—you'll find all manner
of garish marvels calculated to lure players away from the
competition. You'll also see more money changing hands
faster than you've ever imagined, amid a full range of
human emotion from euphoria to despair: high drama
that makes for world-class people-watching.

There are two casino districts. The Strip, on and near
which all the major resort hotels are located, is Las Vegas
Boulevard South, from the 2000 block (just north of Sahara Avenue) to the Hacienda at the 3900 block. Downtown casinos center on Fremont Street west of Las Vegas
Boulevard, commonly known as Glitter Gulch. Fremont
Street has some fine hotels, most notably the luxurious
Union Plaza, as well as small sleazy casinos where huck-
sters lure players off the sidewalk with free-play coupons,
and lights so bright you can take photos at night without
a flash. Las Vegas consumes more electricity per capita
than any other community in the world. Any one of the
major Strip or downtown casino hotels uses more electricity than the entire city of Santa Fe, New Mexico.

Lodging

Las Vegas offers good hotel room bargains in all price
ranges. However, if you're arriving without reservations,
you may quickly discover that the city is booked to
capacity in advance on weekends and fills up almost
every weekday evening.

The following price ranges are approximate, since
room rates change constantly according to demand, and
most hotels will not guarantee prices on advance reserva-

tions. It is difficult to find one-night reservations for
Saturday night only. Rates are always lower Sunday
through Thursday.

Las Vegas's top traditional luxury hotel is **Caesars Palace**, 3750 Las Vegas Boulevard South, toll-free (800)
634-6661; rates for doubles are about $105 to $160. As
opulent as Caesars Palace is the newest hotel on the Strip,
the **Mirage**, 3400 Las Vegas Boulevard South. Room rates
run from $79 on weekdays to $159 on weekends. For
reservations, call toll-free (800) 627-6667. A close com-
petitor when it comes to elegance in casino hotels is
Bally's-Las Vegas, formerly the MGM Grand Hotel, at
3645 Las Vegas Boulevard South, toll-free (800) 634-3434.
Rooms at Bally's cost $84 to $175. Reservations at Bally's
can also be made through Las Vegas Hotel Reservations,
(800) 446-5708, which also books rooms for the
Flamingo Hilton ($72 to $122), and the **Riviera** ($59 to
$95) on the Strip, as well as the **Las Vegas Hilton** ($80 to
$170) near the convention center and the **Union Plaza**
($30 to $50) and **Lady Luck** ($39 to $75) hotels downtown. Other midrange casino hotels include the New
Orleans-style **Four Queens**, 202 East Fremont Street
(downtown), toll-free (800) 634-6045, $47 to $57; and
Circus Circus, 2880 Las Vegas Boulevard South, toll-free
(800) 634-6833 from Arizona, California, Utah, or Idaho,
(800) 634-3450 from other states, $30 to $44; and the
medieval-theme **Excalibur**, 3850 Las Vegas Boulevard
South, (702) 597-7777, $39 to $69.

The lowest room prices on the Strip—$32 to $36—are
at the **Motel Monaco**, 3073 Las Vegas Boulevard South,
(702) 735-9222. Low-cost accommodations are also available at the **Somerset House Motel**, 294 Convention
Center Drive, (702) 735-4411, a block west of the Landmark and two blocks from the convention center. All
rooms cost $36 weekdays, $40 weekends, and you take
your chances: some rooms are budget basic, while others
are suite-sized with full kitchen facilities.

One of the most luxurious hotels in Las Vegas has no
casino. The **Alexis Park Resort Inn**, 375 E. Harmon

Avenue, (702) 796-3300, is located well away from the
strip, convenient to the university and airport. Since Las
Vegas became one of the leading sites in the U.S. for large
conventions, there has been a growing demand for quality accommodations away from the gambling scene. The
Alexis has health club and spa facilities, a putting green,
tennis courts, and three pools. Rates range from $95 to
nearly $600 a night.

Las Vegas has no B&Bs or period restoration hotels. If
the casino hotel scene is not for you, the region's best
historic hotel is **Boulder Dam Hotel**, 1305 Arizona
Street, Boulder City, (702) 293-1808, a reasonably priced
colonial-style 1930s hotel originally built for dignitaries
visiting Hoover Dam, recently renovated, with period
furnishings. Gambling is prohibited in Boulder City.

Camping
Circusland, the 420-site RV campground operated by
Circus Circus, behind the hotel, (702) 734-0410, same
toll-free numbers as the hotel, bills itself as "The World's
Finest RV Park." Well . . . the scenery may leave something to be desired, but it *is* within convenient walking
distance of the "World's Largest Curio Shop." Amenities
include a pool, Jacuzzi, children's playground, laundry
and 24-hour convenience store, and full hookups, $10
per night. An elevated tramway carries campers to the
hotel's casino.

Sightseeing Highlights: Casino Hotels
Some of the more famous Strip casino hotels, such as the
Desert Inn (where Howard Hughes's penthouse was
located) and the Sands (Ronald Reagan's favorite), are
traditional, comparatively dignified country club-style
resorts that feature golf, tennis, and swimming pools but
not much to invite sightseeing by nonguests. Other
casinos will go to any length to attract attention. Here are
the most unusual sights on and near the Strip, from north
to south:

▲ **Bob Stupak's Vegas World**—It's the one with the big silver rocket in front. See the building-size mural of the moon and the earth, and don't miss the fiber-optic model of the solar system on the lobby ceiling or the Apollo Skylab replica.

▲▲ **Circus Circus**—Imagine the bizarre burst of creative thought that inspired the construction of this pink and white striped building in the shape of a circus tent, paid for by computers that play poker (and win). Circus Circus was the first casino designed with families in mind. The mezzanine has a midway of carnival games (prizes are offered, but no gambling) and the latest in video games, as well as a merry-go-round bar overlooking the casino. The midway is a good place from which to watch circus acts, which are performed above the casino on the hour from 11:00 a.m. to midnight.

▲ **Las Vegas Hilton**—Easy to spot, several blocks off the Strip and just north of the convention center, the central attraction here is Benihana Village, a Japanese restaurant and lounge complex patterned after a temple courtyard. Light shows and fountains simulate fireworks and thunderstorms. The Imperial Room, the Hilton's French restaurant, displays replicas of the British crown jewels.

▲ **The Landmark**—Midway between the Hilton and the Strip on Convention Center Drive, this instantly recognizable Space Needle-style tower, which Howard Hughes built, affords the best nighttime view of Las Vegas' lights from the lounge, restaurants, and nightclub on the top floors.

▲▲▲ **Mirage**—This new luxury casino hotel, under the same ownership as the Golden Nugget downtown, is located just north of Caesars Palace on the same side of the Strip. You can't miss the "volcano" out front, which erupts nightly and has a man-made waterfall—an astonishing display of conspicuous water consumption in the desert. (The water is recycled from the hotel plumbing system.) Inside, you'll find a 60-foot atrium containing a rain forest and more waterfalls, a European shopping area, and rare, live white tigers owned by magicians Siegfried and Roy, who perform at the hotel regularly.

▲▲▲ **Caesars Palace**—For sheer unabashed spectacle, Caesars Palace is unrivaled. If you visit only one Strip casino, make it this one. Starting from the corner of Flamingo and the Strip, ride the moving sidewalk past fountains, cypress trees, and replicas of ancient statues, as the voice of Caesar urges you on. From the front entrance, go around to the right of the main casino to see Cleopatra's Barge (a full-size replica that serves as a floating dance floor and lounge) and bigger-than-life replicas of two Michelangelo statues. Take a look at the Olympiad Race and Sports Book, with its 19-foot-by-26-foot TV screen plus 19 other TV screens, each showing live coverage of a different sporting event. Farther in the same direction is the Omnimax Theater—movie thrills on a wraparound projection dome. Call 731-7900 for current show information. Around on the west side of the hotel, the pool area, the Garden of the Gods, is a replica of the baths of Pompeii. Peek in if you can't sneak in. Climb the grand staircase for a glimpse into the private rooms where baccarat is played for high stakes. Finally, don't miss the Brahma Shrine, imported from Thailand, on the north lawn. The hotel provides incense and flowers for worshipers. If this shrine seems strangely out of place amid all the macho neo-Romanism, take a look around and see how many Asian tourists visit Las Vegas. Caesars Palace is building a new 150-store retail complex to be known as the Forum. It promises to be the most expensive shopping district in Las Vegas; it will also have an outdoor "Roman Village Bazaar."

▲▲ **Bally's-Las Vegas**—Originally built by MGM motion picture studios as a lavish tribute to an earlier era of big-screen Hollywood opulence, this huge crystal-and-marble grand hotel burned down in 1980 and was rebuilt with even more elegance; then it was sold to Bally's, the corporation that makes slot machines, pinball machines, and video games. The casino is still the largest in town, and the movie house with its romantic loveseats still shows classic films (three showings nightly plus two matinees each weekend day, $4.50 for adults, $3.75 for children under 12, $3 for senior citizens).

▲ **The Dunes**—Amid Arabic ambience, look for the
Xanadunes video game area—all the newest and flashi-
est—by the black-glass domed casino with its neon palm
trees. The Dunes, like the Aladdin and several other Las
Vegas hotels, was purchased recently by Japanese
investors.

▲▲ **Excalibur**—At the extreme south end of the Strip,
past the Tropicana, this new castle hotel designed for
families by the owners of Circus Circus has a lavish King
Arthur's Court theme and nightly jousting tournaments.

Other Sightseeing Highlights
▲ **Museum of Natural History**—On the University of
Nevada-Las Vegas campus, off Tropicana midway between
Paradise Road and Maryland Parkway, the museum features desert exhibits that range from Native American arts
and crafts to dinosaur fossils to live rattlesnakes behind
glass. Open Tuesday through Sunday 9:00 a.m. to 5:00
p.m.; closed Mondays. Admission is $5 for adults, $4 for
senior citizens and students, $2.50 for children under
age 12.

▲ **Liberace Museum**—This monument to conspicuous
consumption is pretty strange even for Las Vegas. See the
late Lee Liberace's piano collection, limousines, furs, and
115,000-karat rhinestone at 1775 East Tropicana, between
Maryland Parkway and Eastern Avenue, east of the Strip.
The museum is open Monday through Saturday from
10:00 a.m. to 5:00 p.m. and Sundays from 1:00 to 5:00
p.m. Admission is $6.50 for adults, $4.50 for those over
age 60, $3.50 for students, and $2 for children age 6
to 12.

▲ **Nevada State Museum and Historical Society**—
Local history as well as plant, animal, and Indian exhibits
are housed in this modern adobe-style building at 700
Twin Lakes Drive, adjoining Lorenzi Park. Take Sahara
Avenue west from the Strip to Valley View Road, turn
north (right) and continue to Bonanza Road, just past the
Las Vegas Expressway. Turn right on Bonanza and you're
there. The museum is open daily from 8:30 a.m. to 4:30

p.m. Admission is $1 for adults, free for people under age 18.

▲ **Las Vegas Art Museum**—Across the park from the state museum, the art museum (built of railroad ties) is a relic from Twin Lakes Resort, which occupied the present-day city park back in the 1920s and 1930s. The museum, exhibiting works by local artists, may help dispel the impression that Las Vegas is a cultural wasteland. Open Tuesday through Saturday from 10:00 a.m. to 4:00 p.m., Sundays from 12:00 noon to 4:00 p.m., closed Mondays; free admission.

▲**Ripley's Believe It or Not! Museum**—Downtown at the Four Queens Hotel, this hall of sensationalism, along with several other Ripley's museums around the United States, has been attracting tourists for forty years. Today it has a certain quaintness. Believe it or not, this is the only place in the Southwest where you can see a real shrunken head. Open Sunday through Thursday from 10:00 a.m. to 12:00 midnight, Friday and Saturday from 9:00 a.m. to 1:00 a.m. Admission is $4.95 for adults, $3.95 for those over 50, and $2.50 for children ages 6 to 12.

▲ **Old Mormon Fort**—This restored fort at Washington and Las Vegas Boulevard was the first settlement in the Las Vegas area, built in 1855 as a way station for travelers between Salt Lake City and Los Angeles. Open Saturday and Monday 8:00 a.m. to 2:00 p.m. and Sunday 12:00 noon to 3:00 p.m. during the summer months, Monday and Saturday 10:00 a.m. to 4:00 p.m. and Sunday 1:00 to 4:00 p.m. the rest of the year; closed Tuesday through Friday. Admission is $1 for adults, $0.50 for children under 12.

▲ **Red Rock Canyon**—If you want to escape Las Vegas's clattering artificiality for a few hours, drive out W. Charlston Boulevard (NV 159) for twenty miles to this popular hiking and picnicking area. A 13-mile scenic loop road takes you through the canyon of red sandstone and gray limestone. Hiking trails lead into mysterious side canyons. Open during daylight hours. Admission is free.

Food

The most self-indulgent dining in Las Vegas, if you can
get reservations, is the lavish **Bacchanal** at Caesars Palace, complete with scantily clad "wine goddesses." The
cost is about $60 per person. Seatings are Tuesday
through Sunday at 6:00 to 6:30 p.m. and 9:00 to 9:30
p.m., closed Mondays. Reservations are required—call
731-7110 or make them at the hotel desk. Also in Caesars
Palace, **Primavera** serves pricey Italian food overlooking
the hotel's Garden of the Gods swimming pool.

Other interesting dining possibilities in the casino
hotels include **Tracy's** in Bally's (Continental, open Friday through Tuesday 5:00 to 11:00 p.m.); the **Ming Ter-
race** in the Imperial Palace (Chinese, open 12:00 noon to
12:00 midnight); **The Steak House** in Circus Circus
(American, 5:00 p.m. to 12:00 midnight); and **Benihana
Village** in the Las Vegas Hilton (Japanese, 6:00 to 11:00
p.m.). All casino hotels also have 24-hour coffee shops,
typically with super-efficient waitresses and almost
instant service. Many casinos offer incredibly cheap
breakfasts, $0.69 to $1.99, in efforts to attract the last of
the up-all-night crowd during the morning hours when
business is slow. But the best food bargain in town—
breakfast, lunch, or dinner—is the all-you-can-eat
buffets served at many casino hotels. They run from $4 to
$8, with champagne often served at the more expensive
ones, and because of growing competition they vie in
true Las Vegas style for the "most sumptuous spread"
title. Look for buffets at Caesars Palace, the Mirage,
Bally's, the Imperial Palace, Circus Circus, the Flamingo
Hilton, or any of several other Strip casinos. They are
often advertised on the hotels' marquees. Outside of the
hotels, local favorite Las Vegas restaurants include **Bat-
tista's Hole in the Wall**, a moderately priced Italian restaurant known as a show business hangout, behind
Bally's at 4041 Audrie Street, open nightly 5:00 to 11:00
p.m., reservations essential—call 732-1424; the **Star-
board Tack**, serving steaks and seafood in the most nau-
tical ambience to be found in the whole Mojave Desert at

2601 Atlantic Avenue (off Sahara one block east of Eastern), 457-8794, open Monday through Friday from 11:30 a.m. to 6:00 a.m. and Friday and Saturday from 5:00 p.m. to 6:00 a.m.; and **Flakey Jake's**, which offers the biggest build-it-yourself hamburgers in town at 2870 S. Maryland Parkway (east of the Strip between Desert Inn Road and E. Sahara Avenue), open 11:00 a.m. to 10:00 p.m. daily.

Ethel M Chocolates Factory at 2 Cactus Garden Drive, Henderson (take Tropicana Boulevard east and watch for signs; there is also a retail outlet downtown), 452-7805, makes delicious liqueur-filled chocolates that are only sold in Nevada. Epicures everywhere lust for them. The candy factory was started by the late Ethel Mars, who invented Mars Bars and M&Ms, then retired here to create masterpieces. Take the free tour, try a few samples, and soon you'll have to figure out what to do with boxes of chocolates in 100-degree heat. Hint: take them back to your air-conditioned hotel room. Then eat them.

Shows and Nightlife

In addition to free lounge acts (from rising stars to nearly laughable also-ran crooners) just off the casino floor, all major casino hotels have showrooms where performances are generally priced from $20 to $50 (including dinner at the early show around 8:00 p.m. or drinks at the midnight show). Las Vegas hotels pay performers higher than any other nightclubs in the nation, and big names and flawless big-budget productions are everywhere up and down the Strip. On any given night you'll face a choice of entertainers ranging from longtime Vegas favorites like Wayne Newton, Tony Bennett, Neil Diamond, and Englebert Humperdinck to famous "newcomers" like Dolly Parton, Eddie Murphy, the Neville Brothers, and Alabama. In addition to frequently changing big-name performers, many hotels stage permanent "extravaganzas" full of chorus lines, special effects, and elaborate sets and costumes. Among them are Bally's *Jubilee*, the Tropicana's *Folies Bergere*, the Stardust's *Lido de Paris*, and the Riviera's *An Evening at La Cage*. The best magic shows anywhere are in Las Vegas; don't pass up a chance to see David Copperfield or Siegfried and Roy if they're in town when you are.

Most shows change frequently. Schedules and reservations are available three to four months in advance from the Las Vegas Chamber of Commerce, 2301 East Sahara, (702) 457-5544. (Most travel agents around the nation can also provide Las Vegas show schedules.) On short notice, it is easiest to get tickets for the show at the hotel where you are staying. Entertainment schedules are published in the Thursday *Las Vegas Sun* and Friday *Las Vegas Review-Journal* newspapers.

Most cultural events (sponsored by the Las Vegas Arts Alliance) and rock concerts are held at the University of Nevada-Las Vegas. Performance information is available 24 hours a day by calling 739-3131.

A Word about Gambling

Many casinos offer "fun books," coupons you get from the cashier by showing an out-of-state driver's license along with a flyer distributed at tourist information booths, service stations, and restaurants outside Clark County. The books lure you with offers of freebies ranging from breakfast to candy and cocktails, discounts on rooms, meals, and shows, and free play on certain slot machines. Some of these special free-play machines have the odds rigged in your favor—to let you win. Free money? Don't bet on it. The house knows that once you start gambling, it doesn't matter how much of their money you win. They've got plenty more. You'll keep playing until you lose your money. ("Not me," everybody says until they try it.) That phenomenon of human nature keeps Las Vegas residents employed and pays for all the ostentation and electricity.

Besides the loudest wallpaper on earth (designed by experts to drive you out of the room and down to the casino), hotel guest rooms feature "how to gamble" programming on closed-circuit TV. For visitors who are ready to move up from slot machines and video poker to higher-stakes games of chance, several casinos offer free gambling classes. The Imperial Palace has a fourth-floor gambling school where you can practice with fake chips—roulette and blackjack lessons at 9:00 a.m. and 1:00 p.m., craps at 11:00 a.m. and 3:00 p.m. Other hotels such as the Riviera, the Tropicana, and both Hiltons give gambling instruction in special areas of the casino. The Las Vegas Hilton will show you how baccarat works, and the Frontier teaches poker. Advance registration is not necessary, and the lessons are free (in a manner of speaking).

Gaming revenues in Las Vegas exceed $2 billion per year. That's nearly $4,000 a year for each man, woman, and child in the city. Visitors' gambling losses average $154.

ARIZONA'S WEST COAST

After the Colorado River spills through the huge generators at Hoover Dam, it continues into a series of other
dams and reservoirs. None of these desert lakes is anywhere near the size of Lake Powell or Lake Mead. In most
places, they still look like a river—but a deep, lazy river as
wide as the Mississippi, nothing like the whitewater tor-
rent that crashes through the Grand Canyon a hundred or
so miles upriver. Hoover Dam tamed the river. The other
dams and resort towns downstream use it. As much as
one-third of the water in the Colorado River evaporates
from the surface of the manmade lakes as it makes its way
through the harsh, sun-baked Mohave Desert. The rest is
diverted to irrigate farmland in southern California. By
the time the river reaches the Mexican border and the
delta where it used to flow into the Sea of Cortés, there is
no water left in it.

Suggested Schedule

9:00 a.m.	Leave Las Vegas.
10:30 a.m.	Cross Davis Dam into Arizona at Laughlin/Bullhead City.
12:00 noon	Arrive in Lake Havasu City. Lunch by London Bridge. Maybe a boat cruise?
2:00 p.m.	Leave Lake Havasu City and drive to Oatman.
3:30 p.m.	Visit Oatman.
4:30 p.m.	Drive to Kingman or Laughlin.
5:00 p.m.	Check into your accommodations at Kingman or Laughlin, or camp at Hualapai Mountain Park.

Travel Route: Las Vegas to Kingman via Lake Havasu City (242 miles)

From Las Vegas, take US 93 southbound for 23 miles to
Boulder City. Turn south on US 95, where the sign says
"Searchlight/Needles." Go 54 miles south on this high-

Las Vegas to Kingman

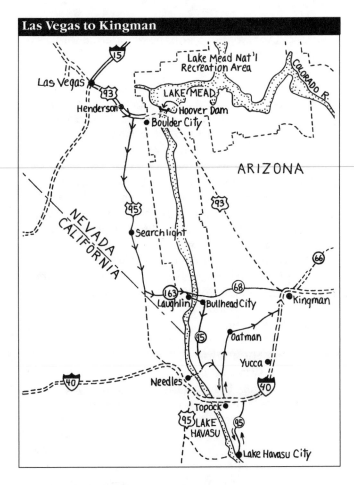

way, through the stark rocky hills and dry lakebeds of the Mohave Desert, and turn left (east) on NV 163. It's 21 miles to Davis Dam, which contains Lake Mohave, the next Colorado River reservoir south of Lake Mead. The casino strip of Laughlin is 3 miles below the dam on the Nevada side.

Cross the dam into Arizona. Because Arizona does not believe in Daylight Savings Time, you change time zones here in the winter but not in the summer. As you cross the dam, NV 163 becomes AZ 68. Turn south on AZ 95

(State Highway 95, which follows the east bank of the Colorado River, *not* U.S. 95 on the Nevada/California side of the river). Bullhead City is 3 miles south of Davis Dam on the Arizona side.

Continue south on AZ 95 for 39 miles to Topock, where it joins Interstate 40. Take the interstate east for two exits (about 9 miles) and exit south on AZ 95. It is 21 miles from the interstate to Lake Havasu City.

Upon leaving Lake Havasu City, retrace your route north to I-40 and Topock. Take AZ 95 for 4 miles north from Topock. Where the road forks near Golden Shores Marina, take a right. From there, the narrow, crumbling paved road that, incredibly, was once part of Route 66, the main highway to southern California, goes about 20 miles to Oatman, then another 27 miles over the crest of a small mountain range to return to I-40 at Kingman.

If you plan to stay in Laughlin tonight, the more direct way to get back there from Kingman is to take AZ 68 due west for 28 miles to the river, a spectacular trip through a lunar landscape.

Sightseeing Highlights

▲ **Bullhead City and Laughlin**—With a population of more than 25,000, Bullhead City is the fastest-growing city in Arizona. It has warm weather in winter and a great location for fishing and boating on the river between Lake Mohave and Lake Havasu. The community's only industry is casino hotels, located on the Nevada side of the river in Laughlin, a town without residential or commercial areas. The casinos, hotels, and restaurants of Laughlin provide most of the employment not only for Bullhead City but also for residents of Kingman, Arizona, and Needles, California.

Laughlin casinos make most of their money on weekends, when people arrive from Phoenix, just four hours away. On weekdays, this fast-growing casino row caters primarily to motor home travelers, for whom the miles and miles of free RV parking lots (no facilities) make Laughlin much easier than Las Vegas. If you've just come from Las

Vegas, you'll find Laughlin anticlimactic, though the whole casino row fronts on the Colorado River with a beachfront that any Las Vegas hotel might envy. Old-timers say Laughlin reminds them of Las Vegas in the 1950's.

▲ **Lake Havasu State Park**—Almost all of the Arizona shore of Lake Havasu is a state park, with campgrounds, boat ramps, and small swimming beaches at Windsor Beach and Crystal Beach, right in Lake Havasu City, as well as at Cattail Cove, 15 miles south of town. The scenic Mohave Sunset Trail runs for 2 miles between Windsor Beach and Crystal Beach, over rocky desert ridgelines and through dense riverside stands of tamarisk. Fifteen miles south of town, there are more camping, boating, and water sports facilities at Cattail Cove. Besides these areas, the park takes in the Aubrey Hills Natural Area, a wild shoreline that can't be reached by road.

Boat rentals are available in Lake Havasu City (contact Island Boat Rentals, 1580 Dover Avenue, 453-3260; Lake Havasu Marina, 1100 McCulloch Boulevard, 855-2159; or Resort Boat Rentals, English Village, 453-9613). Many excursion boats also cruise the lake from London Bridge. Canoes are for rent in Topock at the Jerkwater Canoe Company (768-7753) to explore the Havasu-Topock National Wildlife Refuge at the north end of the lake.

▲▲ **London Bridge**—Lake Havasu City (pop. 25,000) is "the most successful free-standing new town in the United States," according to the *Los Angeles Times*. It was founded less than thirty years ago by two partners, chain-saw king Robert McCulloch and developer C. V. Wood, Jr., who had recently retired from his position as general manager of Disneyland. Carefully planning each smallest detail of their dream community, they decided that they needed a tourist attraction to lure visitors off the inter-state and prime the local economy. So they bought the London Bridge, which was being replaced and auctioned off by the city of London.

The bridge, built in 1825 to replace a still older London

Bridge, is the same one Charles Dickens and Sir Arthur
Conan Doyle wrote about. After buying it for $2,460,000,
McCulloch and Wood disassembled it into stone blocks
weighing from 1,000 to 17,000 pounds of each, then
transported the 10,000 tons of granite for 10,000 miles to
reassemble it on the shore of Lake Havasu. Finally, they
dredged a canal to let water flow under the bridge. Most
onlookers scoffed at the time, seeing the London Bridge
project as the all-time greatest folly ever perpetrated by a
land developer. But it worked. Today, the London Bridge
is the second-most-popular tourist attraction in Arizona,
surpassed only by the Grand Canyon. You can drive
across the bridge or walk across. It's open 24 hours a day,
and it's free.

▲▲ **Oatman**—Some towns just won't die. The gold
boomtown of Oatman thrived from 1906 to 1942, when
the mines closed. It could easily have dried up and blown
away like its sister community, Goldroad, a few miles up
the highway, where buildings were pulled apart for fire-
wood and demolished to the foundations to reduce property taxes. But Oatman's buildings were saved thanks to
motion picture companies who preserved it as a location
for cowboy movies. Today, tourism keeps Oatman going.
Wild burros, descendents of animals who worked in the
mines, wander the streets of town panhandling for
snacks. Oatman gets lively on weekends with bluegrass
music and mock shootouts in the streets. The most interesting sight in town is the funky "honeymoon suite" in
the old Oatman Hotel, where Clark Gable and Carol Lom-
bard spent their wedding night en route back to Hollywood after their surprise marriage ceremony in Kingman.

▲ **Mohave Museum of History and Arts**—Kingman is
the world's leading producer of jewelry-grade turquoise,
and this museum features the Colbaugh Collection of
carved turquoise, some local and more from places as dis-
tant as Persia. The museum also has displays of regional
history from prehistoric times to the present, a miniature
Mohave Indian village diorama, and a room memorializ-
ing Kingman's most famous native son, the late actor

Andy ("Hey, Wild Bill, wait for me!") Devine. Located a quarter-mile east of the Beale Street exit from I-40, the museum is open Monday through Friday from 10:00 a.m. to 5:00 p.m., Saturday and Sunday 1:00 to 5:00 p.m. Admission is $1 for adults, children under 12 free if accompanied by an adult.

▲ **Hualapai Mountain Park**—Think back. When was the last time you saw a pine tree? You'll find cool mountain forests and great scenic views just 14 miles southeast of Kingman on paved Hualapai Mountain Road. This 2,200-acre county park, set at 5,000 feet elevation with mountain peaks rising to 8,000 feet, has picnic grounds and more than ten miles of hiking trails. Abundant wildlife includes deer, elk, and coyotes, as well as many species of birds not often seen in the Mohave Desert.

Camping

Hualapai Mountain Park outside of Kingman has 67 tent campsites for $5 a night and 11 RV sites with hookups for $10 a night. There are drinking water and rest rooms—no showers. The setting, in a shady island of mountain forest above the sunbaked Mohave Desert, is wonderful for evening and early morning walks.

Or camp free at **Wild Cow Campground**, 6 miles past the county park on Hualapai Mountain Road. There are pit toilets but no drinking water or hookups at this 20-site campground operated by the Bureau of Land Management. Open from May through October only.

Food and Lodging

The most interesting accommodations in the Kingman area are at the **Hualapai Mountain Lodge**, (602) 757-3435. The rustic lodge, built at Hualapai Mountain Park by the Civilian Conservation Corps in the 1930s, rents cabins for about $55 a night. There is a restaurant and a grocery store on the premises.

For low-cost luxury lodging, your best bet is to spend the night in Laughlin, Nevada. On Sunday through Thursday nights, spacious, nicely furnished modern rooms at almost any of the ten big casino hotels cost less than accommodations in typical roadside motels in Kingman. The largest hotel in Laughlin is also the oldest, dating back to 1977, when Don Laughlin bought the Riverside Bait Shop, incorporated its site as a town, and expanded it into the 661-room **Riverside Resort**, (702) 298-2535. Rooms run $39 on weeknights, $58 on weekends. At the **Colorado Belle**, (702) 298-4000, a showy hotel built in the shape of a giant riverboat by the same company as Circus Circus and Excalibur in Las Vegas, rates run $27 on weeknights, up to $59 on weekends. Similar rates are available at the **Edgewater**, (702) 298-2453, and **Sam's Town Gold River**, (702) 298-2242 The finest hotel in town, over the crest of a ridge from the rest of casino row, is the Mexican-theme **Harrah's Del Rio**, (702) 298-4600, where rates range from $29 to $50 on week-days, $55 to $90 on weekends. All of these hotels have swimming pools, spas, beaches on the river, and of course gambling casinos. They also have good, inexpensive all-you-can-eat buffets as well as coffee shops and full-service restaurants.

Nightlife
If your travel style includes wine, music, and such, Laughlin is your best bet on the lower Colorado River. All of the casinos have free lounges with live entertainment nightly. The **Riverside Resort** is the only place in town with a Las Vegas-style dinner showroom. They feature big-name acts like the Gatlin Brothers, the Oakridge Boys, and Willie Nelson. Sam's Town Gold River offers **Sandy Hackett's Comedy Club**, where stand-up comics do dinner shows and late shows Wednesday through Saturday nights.

PRESCOTT, JEROME, AND SEDONA

Through western Arizona, old Route 66 followed a different route than today's Interstate 40 does. You drove part
of that route through Oatman yesterday. This morning
you can travel the rest of it (or skip it and take the interstate). The afternoon part of the trip takes you through
two historic old towns—Prescott, the first territorial capital, and Jerome, a once-rich mining town—to end the day
in the contemporary resort community of Sedona. This
route offers a wealth of sightseeing choices ranging from
Indian ruins and exceptional historical museums to hiking trails and lakes.

Suggested Schedule

8:30 a.m.	If you spent the night in Laughlin, drive to Kingman.
9:00 a.m.	From Kingman, follow old Route 66.
11:00 a.m.	Briefly return to Interstate 40, then head south to Prescott.
12:30 p.m.	Lunch in Prescott.
1:00 p.m.	See the Sharlott Hall Museum.
2:30 p.m.	Drive to Jerome.
3:30 p.m.	Explore Jerome.
4:30 p.m.	Drive to Sedona.
5:30 p.m.	Arrive in Sedona. Check into your accom-modations for the night or camp nearby in the Redrock Country.

Travel Route: Kingman via Prescott to Sedona (234 miles)

To take the scenic (but slower) route, stay on AZ 66 as it
parallels the railroad tracks northeast from Kingman. This
alternate route takes 93 miles on a 55-mph two-lane highway to reach Seligman, which is 73 miles down the interstate from Kingman. It takes you among gentle hills on a
historic road where not many vehicles travel these days.

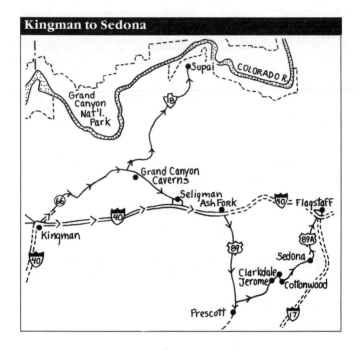

Kingman to Sedona

    The only sightseeing attraction (or sign of recent habi-
tation) along this stretch of old Route 66 is **Grand Canyon Caverns**, a large limestone cave 200 feet underground. The cost of the 45-minute tour is $5.75 for
adults, $3.75 for children ages 6 to 14. As at so many tour-
ist caves, there's a huge dinosaur statue by the entrance.
Near the caverns is the turnoff to Supai (see Itinerary
Options).
    Upon returning to Interstate 40 at Seligman, continue
east for 25 miles to Ash Fork. Exit there on US 89 southbound and drive 52 miles to Prescott. About 6 miles
north of Prescott on US 89, a different highway called US
89A turns east. It goes 58 miles, over the mountains,
through Jerome, to Sedona.

Sightseeing Highlights
▲▲ Prescott—Tucked away between granite hills, Prescott is a lovely little town that seems to be left over from

an earlier era. The first capital of the Arizona Territory, Prescott is one of the oldest towns in the state, dating back to the 1860s. As you stroll down the small-town main street, you may feel that you've been spirited back through time to the 1950s. Wholesome Norman Rockwell-style quaintness coexists with Whisky Row, a notorious block of Old West saloons that are still in operation after all these years. Downtown Prescott is also a good place to shop for antiques.

The major sightseeing attraction in Prescott is the Sharlot Hall Museum, 415 W. Gurley Street, (602) 445-3122. Perhaps Arizona's finest historical museum of the territorial era, this large park contains several nineteenth-century structures, most of which have been moved here from different parts of central Arizona, including two former governor's mansions. There are Victorian furnishings, ranch antiques, Indian artifacts, and a sizeable collection of stagecoaches and other horse-drawn vehicles. The museum is named after its founder, Sharlot Hall. An explorer, essayist, and poet, she became the official historian of Arizona Territory in 1909. Sharlot Hall Museum is open Tuesday through Saturday from 10:00 a.m. to 5:00 p.m. (closing at 4:00 p.m. November through March) and Sunday from 1:00 to 5:00 p.m. year-round. Donations are welcome.

Other highlights, for those who choose to spend extra time exploring Prescott, include the Phippen Museum of Western Art, 4701 US 89 North, which displays works by more than 80 contemporary painters and sculptors (open mid-May through December Monday and Wednesday through Saturday from 10:00 a.m. to 4:00 p.m. and Sunday 1:00 to 4:00 p.m., the rest of the year Wednesday through Monday from 1:00 to 4:00 p.m., Adults $2, seniors $1.50, students ages 12 to 18 $1); The Bead Museum, 140 S. Montezuma Street, on Whisky Row, exhibiting one of the world's largest collections of beads and explaining their many uses throughout history (open Monday through Saturday from 9:30 a.m. to 4:30 p.m., free); and the Smoki Museum, 100 N. Arizona Avenue, displaying a large collection of authentic and spurious

Indian artifacts owned by the Smokis, a local "tribe" of "Wannabe Indians" that has been headquartered in Prescott for 70 years (open during the summer months only, Monday, Tuesday, and Thursday through Saturday from 10:00 a.m. to 4:00 p.m., Sunday 1:00 to 4:00 p.m., adults $2, children under 12 free).

An easy hike from town is the 1.7-mile loop trail that goes from Thumb Butte Park on the edge of town up onto Thumb Butte for good views of the town and the valley. A popular local recreation area is Granite Dells, 4 miles north of town on US 89, which has fantastic rock formations and a fishing lake.

▲▲ **Jerome**—High on a mountainside midway between Prescott and Sedona, Jerome was the site of environmental plunder on a grand scale. Paradoxically, it is now one of the most charming communities in central Arizona. Named after a cousin of Jenny Jerome (Winston Churchill's mother), the town had a population of 15,000 near the end of the nineteenth century, most of the residents living in tents. In 72 years, $800,000,000 worth of copper was dug from the mountainside, along with modest amounts of gold and silver. (Imagine 80 billion pennies. Stacked, they would make a column 63,000 miles tall. Laid in a row, they would reach almost a million miles. You could pave every inch of the U.S. interstate highway system with pennies and have more than a million dollars left over.)

Jerome was destroyed by fire three times in three years (1897-1899). One of the fires, a Prescott newspaper reported, wiped out the entire downtown area, consisting of 24 saloons, 14 Chinese restaurants, several casinos, and the red light district. After the third fire, the town was rebuilt in brick. Jerome was abandoned in 1953 when the mines closed down.

Jerome is a National Historic District. Since the 1960s it has been repopulated, mainly by artists and craftspeople, to a present population of about 500. Visit the Gold King Mine and Museum, the Jerome Historical Society Mine Museum, or the Jerome State Historic Park Museum, but the town's real charm is to be found all along the switchback main street with its folksy array of galleries, eateries, and rock shops.

▲ **Tuzigoot National Monument**—Ruins of a white stone Sinagua Indian pueblo occupied in the ninth through thirteenth centuries stand atop a hill that now overlooks a slag field from the abandoned refinery that used to process the ore from Jerome's mines. The museum at the monument has a fine collection of artifacts found while excavating the site. Tuzigoot National Monument is located off the main highway 2 miles east of Clarkdale. It is open daily in the summer months from 8:00 a.m. to 7:00 p.m., the rest of the year from 8:00 a.m. to 5:00 p.m. Admission is $1 per person.

▲▲ **Sedona**—Perched between blistering desert lowlands and cool mountain forests in the heart of Arizona's Red Rock Country, this booming resort town has grown from a handful of pioneering residents to a year-round population of 12,000 in just twenty years. It has more millionaires per capita than any other municipality in the state, and it is the New Age capital of the known universe. Sedona has no museums or other conventional sightseeing highlights. The top activities are shopping and exploring the spectacular landscape that surrounds the town.

Shoppers will find dozens of galleries, boutiques, and cute little stores throughout uptown Sedona. The most enjoyable place to browse is the large, Spanish Colonial-style Tlaquepaque shop and restaurant complex on AZ 179 south of the "Y" (the junction of highways 179 and 89A).

Besides Oak Creek Canyon (see tomorrow's Sightseeing Highlights), the Sedona area has many wonderful less-known places to experience the wonders of the Red Rock Country. Jeep trails beckon to mountain bikers, and bikes can be rented at several shops in town. Tours by bicycle, four-wheel-drive vehicle, van, or hot-air balloon are available from numerous guide services. Some of Sedona's most popular outdoor spots are known locally as "vortices." These places, according to local New Agers, ooze earth energy that enhances psychic perception, puts channelers in touch with ancient Indian spirits, attracts UFOs, and so forth. Before you scoff, see for yourself by hiking the beautiful 3-mile Boynton Canyon Trail, the most popular "vortex," from Boynton Pass Road, an extension of Dry Creek Road, which leaves US 89A in West Sedona.

Camping

The best camping spots around Sedona are at a series of campgrounds operated by the National Forest Service in Oak Creek Canyon. **Manzanita Campground**, 6 miles north of Sedona, has 19 sites. **Cave Spring Campground**, 12 miles north of town, has 78 sites, and **Pine Flat Campground**, a mile farther up the canyon, has 58. Fees at all three are $8 a night. All are along the creek. None has RV hookups. These campgrounds are only open from mid-May through mid-September, and they are crowded all summer. If no sites are available here, look for campgrounds in the Flagstaff area (see tomorrow's listings).

Lodging

Most accommodations in the Sedona area are upscale. Among the best are **L'Auberge de Sedona**, 301 L'Auberge Lane, (602) 282-7131, a French Provincial-style country inn in a secluded creekside location within walking distance of the center of town ($140 to $165), and **Los Abrigados**, 160 Portal Lane, (602) 282-1777, a large luxury resort situated immediately behind the Tlaquepaque complex ($185 to $235). Relatively low-priced lodging can be found in Sedona at the **Matterhorn Motor Lodge**, 230 Apple Avenue, (602) 282-7176 ($64 to $69) or the **Sedona Motel**, SR 179 one block south of the "Y," (602) 282-7187 ($54 to $59).

In Oak Creek Canyon, several clusters of cabins near Slide Rock State Park rent for around $90 a night. Try **Slide Rock Cabins** (602-282-6900), **Don Hoel's Cabins** (602-282-3560), or **Forest Houses** (602-282-2999).

Travelers seeking budget-priced accommodations should plan to spend the night in Flagstaff (see tomorrow's listings).

Food

For lunch in Prescott, **Greens and Things**, 106 W. Gurley Street, 445-3234, serves salads, omelets, and homemade soups. The low-budget **Dinner Bell Café**, 321 W. Gurley Street, 445-9888, may not look like much, but it is one of the most popular restaurants in central Arizona.

Stop for a croissant or scone and a cup of gourmet coffee in Jerome at **Macy's European Coffeehouse and Bakery**, Main Street at Hull, 634-2733.

In Sedona, you can find one of the finest (and priciest) dinners of your whole Southwest trip at the **Oak Creek Owl**, 561 Highway 179, 282-3532, which specializes in New Southwest cuisine such as shrimp in chile sauce and quail stuffed with pion nuts. Another excellent, expensive restaurant is **Rene at Tlaquepaque**, 282-9225, serving traditional French cuisine in an Old Mexico atmosphere.

Look for basic, affordable food in West Sedona (along US 89A west of the "Y"). **Phil and Eddie's Diner** (1655 West Highway 89A, 282-6070) serves breakfast all day and cheeseburgers along with 1950s drive-in ambience.

Itinerary Options

Shortly before Grand Canyon Caverns on old Route 66 is a turnoff marked "Supai." What the sign doesn't mention is that the isolated Indian village of Supai is down in Havasu Canyon, a branch of the Grand Canyon. On the Supai road, the pavement ends 62 miles from the turnoff. Eleven miles later, at Hualapai Hilltop, the road ends, and it's another 8 miles by foot trail, descending 2,000 feet, to Supai. The trail continues to Havasu Falls and the Colorado River. Consider this trek if you're a serious hiker with plenty of extra time (at least two days) and a desire to hike into the Grand Canyon. Backpacker camping is

allowed only in two tribal campgrounds ($7) along
Havasu Creek. Supai has a café, a food store, and a post
office as well as a lodge ($35 double). You must pay the
tribe an $8 entrance fee upon arrival in Supai. Reserva-
tions are essential, even for camping. Contact Havasupai
Tourist Enterprise, Supai, AZ 86435, (602) 448-2121.

FLAGSTAFF

Flagstaff, just 2½ highway hours from the big city of Phoenix and 1½ from Grand Canyon Village on the South Rim, is northern Arizona's tourist hub. Don't bother moving your campsite or changing motel rooms. Within a few minutes' drive from the city are enough unusual and enjoyable attractions to fill your whole day and then some.

Suggested Schedule

9:00 a.m.	Breakfast.
10:00 a.m.	See Walnut Canyon National Monument.
12:00 noon	Lunch in downtown Flagstaff.
1:15 p.m.	Lowell Observatory (1:30 tour).
	Spend the night in Flagstaff or at a campsite near Sunset Crater.

Flagstaff

The largest city on I-40 west of Albuquerque, Flagstaff (pop. 40,000) was founded in 1881 as a railroad town (the railroad actually reached Flagstaff in 1882). The University of Northern Arizona strikes a cultural counterpoint to Flagstaff's tourist-and-truck-stop aspect.

Historic downtown Flagstaff is at the extreme west end of town. Don't be put off by the trackside heavy industry you see from the interstate or the motel strip business route. Downtown Flagstaff, between Humphreys and Agassiz streets due north of the railroad station on Santa Fe Avenue, is a low-key, low-priced, and generally underrated historic district. Stroll it.

Sightseeing Highlights

▲▲ **Oak Creek Canyon**—The scenic, very popular 27-mile canyon drive from Sedona to Flagstaff climbs from red rock desert to cool ponderosa forest. In July and August as well as early October (autumn colors),

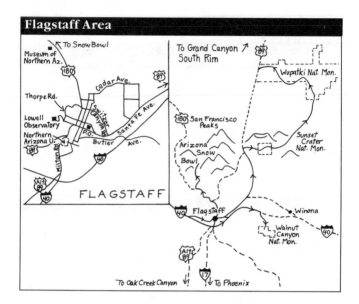

Flagstaff Area

don't expect to find a parking place in any of the canyon's picnic areas or campgrounds.

Slide Rock State Park, midway up the canyon on your left, has traditionally been the local "beach" for students from the University of Northern Arizona in Flagstaff. Now a state park, it has become a little more regulated, not quite as wild as before but just as wet. The creek flows through a series of large, placid pools and down thrilling spillways, flanked by a flat red sandstone shoreline where sunbathers can stretch out. Also in the park is an abandoned 1920s homestead with apple orchards. Picking the fruit is prohibited, but cider made from the apples is sold at a stand near the swimming area. The park is open during daylight hours. Admission is $3 for adults, $1.50 for children ages 12 and under.

▲▲ **Walnut Canyon National Monument**—Just 3 miles off the interstate from exit 204 east of town, Walnut Canyon offers a one-hour walk on a paved trail around an "island" above the canyon to see about a hundred small 800-year-old cliff dwellings of the Sinagua Indians. Look-but-don't-touch views of the pristine wooded canyon floor enhance the experience. Open 7:00 a.m. to 7:00 p.m. Memorial Day to Labor Day, 8:00 a.m. to 5:00 p.m. the rest of the year. Admission is $3 per vehicle.

▲▲ **Lowell Observatory**—Follow the winding road from the west end of Santa Fe Avenue up to this hilltop observatory, founded by wealthy Boston businessman-turned-astronomer Percival Lowell in 1894, just 13 years after Flagstaff became a town. Lowell is best remembered for "discovering" the (nonexistent) canals of Mars and hypothesizing an ancient Martian civilization. One may wonder whether Indian ruins around Flagstaff helped guide his vivid imagination. Based on Lowell's theoretical predictions of a ninth planet, Dr. Clyde Tombaugh discovered Pluto from this observatory in 1930. The "red shift" of galaxies, on which the theory of the expanding universe is based, was also discovered here. Lowell's original telescope in its old wooden observatory tower looks like an antique left over from a Victorian science fiction novel, ideal for Martian-watching. The visitors center is open June through August only, Tuesday through Saturday, 10:00 a.m. to 4:30 p.m. Tours start at 10:00 a.m. and 1:30 p.m. June through September, 1:30 p.m. only the rest of the year. You can look through the telescope between 8:00 and 10:00 p.m. on any Friday night June through August or the first night of any other month. Suggested donations are $1 per person or $3 per family. For pre-recorded information, call 774-2096.

▲ **Museum of Northern Arizona**—This museum, located 3 miles north of downtown Flagstaff on US 180, houses one of the most comprehensive archaeology, ethnology, geology, biology, and fine arts collections in the Southwest. In July, the annual Hopi and Navajo Craftsman Exhibitions draw visitors and collectors from all over the United States. The museum is open daily from 9:00 a.m. to 5:00 p.m. Admission is $3 for adults, $1.50 for ages 5 to 21.

▲ **The Arboretum at Flagstaff**—Arizona flora native to the alpine tundra, evergreen forest, and high desert are exhibited here. Guided tours are Monday through Friday,

starting regularly from 10:00 a.m. to 3:00 p.m. Follow old
Route 66 from South Milton near downtown, turning left
on unpaved Woody Mountain Road, a total distance of
about 4 miles.

▲ **Fairfield Snow Bowl**—In the San Francisco Peaks,
this is the state's highest and best winter downhill ski area
and a popular summer hiking trailhead. In the summer
months, the chair lift carries sightseers to the summit of
Mt. Humphries (11,500 ft.) for a spectacular view of Flagstaff, Sunset Crater/Wupatki, the surrounding forest and
volcano fields, and the Grand Canyon in the distance. Follow US 180 for 7 miles north from Flagstaff, then turn
right and go another 7 miles on an unpaved road. The lift
operates from 10:00 a.m. until 4:00 p.m. in the summer
months, weekends only in September and October. Tickets cost $7 for adults, $3.50 for senior citizens and children ages 6 to 12.

▲▲ **Sunset Crater National Monument**—Thousand-
foot-tall Sunset Crater is the most impressive of about a
dozen volcano cones that dot the forest north of Flagstaff
and west of San Francisco Peaks. These volcanoes are
remarkable because they are so new. Sunset Crater began
erupting in the winter of A.D. 1064-65 and continued to
spew cinders for almost two centuries until A.D. 1250, just
an eyeblink ago in geological time. Today, scientists and
tourists alike watch in suspense for rare, foreboding rum-
bles on the seismograph in the visitors center.

Sunset Crater is no longer very accessible to hikers.
The volcano cone itself is closed to hiking (increased
tourist traffic made too many unsightly footprints across
the cinders); an ice cave, which was the second-best
attraction, collapsed a few years ago. Today, only a short
nature trail is open for walking. From the visitors center,
rangers guide an assortment of other hikes as well as jeep
trips up nearby O'Leary Crater outside the monument.
Combined admission to Sunset Crater and Wupatki
national monuments is $3 per vehicle.

▲▲ **Wupatki National Monument**—Farming Indians
who lived in pithouses here in the eleventh century aban-

doned the area when Sunset Crater began to erupt. When
the fireworks stopped, the porous volcanic ash retained
water for better farming. Indians from several cultures—
Kayenta Anasazi, Sinagua, Hohokam, and Cohonina—
resettled the area. The assortment of architecture and
artifacts found within just a few miles is an archaeologist's field day.

Camping

To reach Coconino National Forest's **Bonito Campground**, across from the visitors center at the south
boundary of Sunset Crater, take the third Flagstaff exit
(#201) and turn north on US 89. Go 10 miles to the turnoff for Sunset Crater National Monument. Bonito Campground is on your left at the monument boundary, across
the road from the Sunset Crater visitors center.

The campground is large, popular, and remarkably spacious. It often fills by 6:00 p.m., so stake out your campsite early, before taking the Sunset Crater-Wupatki drive.
Volunteers from the National Monument present campfire talks nightly during the summer months. From the
upper end of the campground, you can easily walk a mile
or more over the cinder fields along the edge of the jag-
ged lava flow, finding several good views of the lava and
of O'Leary Crater. An unpaved road starts just east of the
campground and goes 5 miles to the summit of the
volcano.

Lodging

The **Hotel Weatherford**, (602) 774-2731, at the corner
of N. Leroux Street and Aspen Avenue, a block north of
the railroad station in downtown Flagstaff, was the most
elegant hotel in town when it opened in 1897. Now a
youth hostel, the Weatherford also offers several rather
spartan private hotel rooms for under $30 double. For the
young at heart, the absence of guest room decor is more
than compensated for by the lively social scene. An international crowd of mostly young travelers congregates in
the second-floor lobby nightly, while Charly's Pub on

the ground floor is popular among local college students. The adjoining restaurant serves homemade soups, breads, desserts, and good dinners.

Another historic downtown hotel, the **Monte Vista** at 100 N. San Francisco St., (602) 774-6971, offers guest rooms remodeled in 1927 decor. Rates range from $38 to $74 double. **Dierker House**, at 423 W. Cherry, (602) 774-3249, offers bed and breakfast for two at about $40.

The 3-mile I-40 business loop north of downtown is lined with motels. The "brand-name" chain motels range from moderate (around $50 double at the **Super 8**) to expensive (around $75 at **Travelodge Suites**, $85 double at the **Best Western Woodlands Plaza**, $90 at **Little America**). A plethora of independent "ma-and-pa" motels offer much lower rates, typically $25 to $35 double, on marquee signs out front. Cruise the motel strip and pick the place that appeals to you. "No vacancy" problems are unlikely as long as you arrive in Flagstaff by 6:00 p.m.

Food

Flagstaff's student population supports a wide variety of reasonably priced, informal restaurants in the downtown area. For Mexican food, try **El Charro**, 409 S. San Francisco, or the **Burrito Palace** at 10 N. San Francisco. Good Chinese food is served at the **Hong Kong Cafe**, 6 E. Santa Fe Avenue, and the **Grand Canyon Cafe**, 110 E. Santa Fe. For good American food, eat at **Charly's** in the Hotel Weatherford. For fine Continental dining, the intimate place to go in Flagstaff is the **Cottage Place**, a small house two blocks south of downtown at 126 W. Cottage Avenue, open Tuesday through Sunday 5:00 to 9:30 p.m., closed Mondays.

The series of shopping centers along Milton Road (US 89A), which runs south from downtown between the railroad tracks and the interstate, offers a selection of supermarkets. For more specialized food shopping, visit **Winnie's Natural Foods**, downtown at the corner of Santa Fe Avenue and San Francisco Street.

Nightlife

For its size, Flagstaff has a lot of after-dark activities, both cultural and otherwise. Most performing arts events are held at the **Coconino Center for the Arts**, 2300 N. Fort Valley Road, 779-6921, or the **Northern Arizona University School of Performing Arts**, 523-3731. Local performance groups include the Flagstaff Symphony Orchestra, the Coconino Chamber Ensemble, the Flagstaff Master Chorale, the Flagstaff Oratorio Chorus, and the NAU Opera Theatre. For current information, ask at the Flagstaff Visitors Center or tune your radio to the university station, KNAU 88.7 FM.

Popular rock'n'roll clubs in town include **Fiddlestix**, 702 S. Milton Road, 774-6623, and **The Monsoons**, 22 E. Santa Fe Avenue, 773-9923. For jazz, try **Charly's** on the first floor of the Weatherford Hotel. A romantic spot is the **Mad Italian** (known locally as the "Mad I"), 101 S. San Francisco Street, 779-1820.

The hottest saloon in town is the **Museum Club**, 3404 E. Santa Fe Avenue, 526-9434. Better known among locals as the "Zoo Club" (for reasons that will quickly become apparent), the building used to be a trading post and taxidermy shop in Flagstaff's early days and has operated as a night club continuously since 1936. Live music here is country and western, and quite a few legends of country music—Bob Wills and the Texas Playboys, Willie Nelson, Commander Cody and the Lost Planet Airmen—have graced the Museum Club's stage.

THE GRAND CANYON: SOUTH RIM

It's still the same canyon you saw on Day 14. But the South Rim is different. For one thing, there's a big new McDonald's near the main park gates (you'll use a different entrance). En route, tour Sunset Crater and Wupatki national monuments to see some of the Southwest's most striking volcanic landscapes.

Suggested Schedule

9:00 a.m.	Get an early start driving to the South Rim of the Grand Canyon. Campgrounds and lodging there fill up fast.
11:00 a.m.	Visit the Tusayan Museum.
12:00 noon	Arrive at Grand Canyon Village. Check into the campground or lodging, then eat lunch.
1:00 p.m.	Visit the Vistors Center and Yavapai Museum.
3:00 p.m.	Ride the shuttle bus along West Rim Drive.
4:30 p.m.	Watch the mule trip return up Bright Angel Trail.
Evening	Another Grand Canyon sunset.

Travel Route: Flagstaff to Grand Canyon South Rim (121 miles)

From I-40 on the eastern edge of Flagstaff, turn north on US 89. Go 10 miles to the turnoff for Sunset Crater National Monument. From Sunset Crater, a 36-mile road takes you north to the Wupatki visitors center and then through Wupatki National Monument. Rejoining US 89, turn right and go north for about 20 more miles to the intersection with AZ 64. Turn west, and another 55 miles will bring you to Grand Canyon Village.

The entrance fee to the Grand Canyon is $10 per vehicle. Your fee receipt from the North Rim, if paid within the last 7 days, will get you into the South Rim as well.

Sightseeing Highlights
▲▲▲ Grand Canyon National Park: South Rim—

This is one of the most visited places in the national park system. Coming from Sunset Crater and Wupatki, you will enter the park through the less-used gates at the east end of East Rim Drive. On the way to Grand Canyon Village, you will see a replica Hopi watchtower and several well-marked points with spectacular views. Take time to stop at the Tusayan ruin and museum a few miles past the watchtower to learn about the Grand Canyon's Anasazi past, as well as the Yavapai Museum, just before you reach the village, for geology and natural history exhibits. Both are free, open daily from 8:00 a.m. to 6:00 p.m. in the summer months and 9:00 a.m. to 5:00 p.m. the rest of the year. The main visitors center, just past the Yavapai Museum, is open from 8:00 a.m. to 7:00 p.m. during the summer months, until 5:00 p.m. the rest of the year.

Grand Canyon Village is big, congested with visitors, and crammed with concessionaires; the rest of the canyon rim is untouched by development. The West Rim Drive is closed to private vehicles during the summer months but accessible by free park service shuttle buses. The easy, paved South Rim Nature Trail runs 3 ½ miles along the rim between the Yavapai Museum, the hotel area, and the Powell Memorial on West Rim Drive.

The South Rim is most famous for its muleback trips down Bright Angel Trail. The trips are as popular as ever—so popular, in fact, that they are often booked up as much as a year in advance. To make reservations, contact Reservations Department, Grand Canyon National Park Lodge, P.O. Box 699, Grand Canyon, AZ 86023, (602) 638-2401. The cost is $70 per person, including lunch, for the one-day trip midway down the canyon, or $219 per person for an overnight trip to Phantom Ranch down on the river. Those who didn't plan that far ahead can check with the lodge to see if cancellations have created space on the next day's mule trip. You can walk over to the corral and watch the mule trips leave each morning around 9:00 to 9:30 and return around 4:30 or

5:00. You can also hike a portion of the Bright Angel Trail
yourself. Take water. If you hike down this trail in the
morning, you may face hot temperatures on the strenuous climb back up.

Just in case seeing the real thing isn't enough, an IMAX
(semidome wraparound screen) theater in Tusayan near
the main entrance gate, 7 miles south of Grand Canyon
Village, shows a half-hour film that includes rafting and
flying footage. Not to be outdone, the Galaxy 4 theaters
just up the road show four different Grand Canyon
movies in separate viewing areas. Admission to either
place is $6 ($4 for children under 12), the same as the
entrance fee to the real Grand Canyon.

Camping
To stay in the campground at Grand Canyon village, you
must make reservations (at least a month in advance) by
mail through TICKETRON Reservation Office, P.O. Box
617516, Chicago, IL 60661-7516, or by calling (800)
452-1111 and prepaying your camping fee with your Visa
or MasterCard. Fees start at $10. There are private camp-
grounds outside the main gate, 7 miles south of Grand
Canyon Village.

Lodging
The original hotel built on the rim of the Grand Canyon
by Fred Harvey in 1905, **El Tovar** is still the most elegant
of the several hotels in Grand Canyon Village. Room rates
are from $105 to $150. Also on the rim are **Kachina
Lodge** ($86 to $92), **Yavapai Lodge** ($67 to $76), and
Maswik Lodge ($46 to $90). Check-in time at all of the
Grand Canyon Village lodges is 3:30. Reservations should
be made far in advance through Grand Canyon National
Park Lodges, P.O. Box 699, Grand Canyon, AZ 86023,
(602) 638-2631.

If you arrive without reservations and find no vacan-
cies within the park, there is a cluster of large resort
motels just outside the south entrance. Prices are pretty
much the same as at the Grand Canyon Village lodges,
and the view isn't as nice.

Food

Grand Canyon Village has restaurant concessionaires in all price ranges. The main dining room at **El Tovar** serves Continental cuisine nightly from 5:00 to 10:00 p.m. as well as breakfast (6:30 to 11:00 a.m.) and luncheon (11:30 a.m. to 2:00 p.m.). There is also a steak house, a hamburger restaurant, a snack bar, and a campers' grocery store.

THE HOPI MESAS

From the well-developed industrial tourism of the Grand
Canyon South Rim, travel this afternoon to one of the
earth's loneliest corners—the traditional mesa-top villages of the Hopi, who have lived there since the peak of
the Anasazi civilizations at Chaco and Mesa Verde.

Suggested Schedule

9:00 a.m.	Breakfast at El Tovar dining room and a leisurely morning gazing at the Grand Canyon.
12:00 noon	After lunch, leave the park and drive to Tuba City on the Navajo Reservation.
2:00 p.m.	At Tuba City, turn off toward the Hopi mesas.
4:00 p.m.	Visit Hopi Cultural Center. Check into your motel room or arrange to camp. Eat dinner at the cultural center.
6:00 p.m.	Stroll the mesa. Listen to the silence.

Travel Route: Grand Canyon Village to Second Mesa (177 miles)

Leave the Grand Canyon the same way you came in,
along East Rim Drive and through the east entrance gate.
Retrace yesterday's route to the intersection with US 89, a
distance of 55 miles. Turn north on US 89 and go 16
miles, then turn east on US 160. Ten miles will bring you
to Tuba City. Turn south there on AZ 264. A 57-mile drive
will bring you to Oraibi, westernmost of the Hopi mesa
villages, on Third Mesa. Continue on the same roller-
coaster highway to the Hopi Cultural Center on Second
Mesa.

The Hopi

When other Anasazi groups abandoned their desert
pueblos and moved to the Rio Grande Valley, the Hopi

stayed in their mesa-top villages. The mesa contains an underground aquifer that has sustained the Hopi people's small, sandy fields—separate patches for red, white, blue, and yellow corn, all planted 18 inches deep—for a thousand years. The most remote of the Pueblo people, they were less influenced by missionaries than other ancient communities like Ácoma were. As recently as the end of World War II, when the first school was built at Keams Canyon, no Hopi spoke English. About that time, curious scientists, writers, artists, photographers, and sightseers began visiting the Hopi mesas, sometimes disrupting kachina and snake dances until finally outsiders were banned from most Hopi ceremonies.

Hopi villagers have a way of making sightseers feel invisible. This is not hostility; it's just a helpful tool for maintaining an eleventh-century agrarian culture in the 1990s. You can drive to most of the villages and wander freely. If you're interested in buying pottery, women who make and sell it may let you look inside their studios. All photography and sketching is strictly prohibited.

On Third Mesa, Old Oraibi has still-occupied homes that date back to about A.D. 1125, making it the oldest continuously inhabited community in the United States. The village is often off-limits to the public, but at other unpredictable times, visitors are admitted for a small fee.

On Second Mesa, at the Hopi Cultural Center, you'll find excellent exhibits on Hopi customs and crafts. The center is open Monday through Friday from 8:00 a.m. to 5:00 p.m. MST, Saturdays from 9:00 a.m. to 4:00 p.m., and, during the summer months only, on Sundays from 10:00 a.m. to 4:00 p.m. (see About Time, below). The fixed-price Hopi arts and crafts shops nearby are a good place to buy quality work. Shungopavi, the tribal religious center, and the smaller Second Mesa villages Shipaulovi and Mishongnovi, were all built around A.D. 1700 by people who had formerly lived below the mesa. The ruins of a previous village, Maseeba, can be seen from an overlook at Shungopavi.

Polacca is a twentieth-century village. Walpi, on the

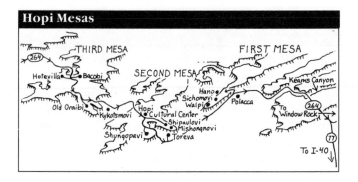

Hopi Mesas

tip of First Mesa, dates back to about A.D. 1400. Two eighteenth-century villages, Sichomovi and Hano— the latter formed by immigrant Pueblo people who fled from New Mexico after the Pueblo Revolt of 1680—are suburbs of Walpi.

Camping
Camp on the Hopi Reservation at the free **Second Mesa Campground and Trailer Park** next to the Cultural Center. You won't find water or hookups, but you can use the rest rooms and other services at the center. Other campgrounds are located below the mesas at **Keams Canyon** and at **Kykotsmovi**, a mile east of New Oraibi.

Lodging
The motel at the Hopi Cultural Center, Box 67, Second Mesa, AZ 86034, (602) 734-2401, has modern rooms with cable TV at about $55 double. Reservations are recommended.

Food
The restaurant at the **Hopi Cultural Center**, the only one on the reservation, features traditional Hopi dishes such as lamb stew, bean soup, and blue corn pancakes. Open daily from 6:30 a.m. to 9:00 p.m. in the summer months, until 8:00 p.m. the rest of the year.

About Time
The Hopi Reservation, like most of Arizona, does not observe daylight saving time. The Navajo Nation, which

completely surrounds the Hopi Reservation, does. If you wanted to be sure you know the exact time, you'd need to set your watch forward an hour when entering Navajo land, then back an hour when you cross onto Hopi land; tomorrow, you'll set it forward an hour when crossing back onto Navajo land, then back an hour when you leave the reservation, and forward an hour when you enter New Mexico. Fortunately, today's and tomorrow's route is in the "Indian time" zone; what your watch says doesn't matter anyway.

DAY 22

THE PETRIFIED FOREST AND ZUÑI COUNTRY

This long driving day will take you through the painted desert country of eastern Arizona, then back to New Mexico in the land of the Zuñi. This afternoon, visit a place where every expedition that passed through New Mexico for 200 years left its mark in stone alongside petroglyphs of the Anasazi before them. Later on, see the volcano fields of El Malpais or take a late afternoon side trip to Ácoma, the most beautiful of all Indian pueblos.

Suggested Schedule

8:00 a.m.	Leave for the Petrified Forest.
10:30 a.m.	Arrive at Petrified Forest National Park. See the hard woods and rainbow sands.
12:00 noon	Leave for El Morro.
3:00 p.m.	Arrive at El Morro National Monument. Find a campsite (or drive on to Grants for lodging tonight).
4:00 p.m.	Visit Bandera Crater and Ice Caves
5:00 p.m.	Check into your Grants lodging or camp at El Morro.
Tomorrow	You're now just two hours from Albuquerque, where you started this journey three weeks ago. Can you resist the temptation to call in sick, take an extra vacation day, and visit Ácoma Pueblo today?

Travel Route: Second Mesa to Grants (325 miles)
Continue on AZ 264 over First Mesa, through Keams Canyon, a total distance of 39 miles to the turnoff for Tribal Route 6, which becomes AZ 77 and goes to Holbrook, 59 miles to the south. There are no towns along this route. You will reach I-40 just east of Holbrook. After stopping in town for gasoline if necessary, proceed eastbound on I-40 for 25 miles to the Petrified Forest entrance.

After the 27-mile drive through the Petrified Forest, exit at the far end of the park on US 180 and drive 36 miles east across empty, arid rangeland to St. Johns. Turn north on US 666 and drive north for 29 miles to the turn-off for AZ 61 on your right. A few miles east, AZ 61 changes into NM 53. Stay on that road, admiring the pink cliffs of the Zuñi Mountains, for 30 miles to the town of Zuñi and about 40 more miles to El Morro National Monument.

As you continue east on NM 53 for the 40-mile drive from El Morro National Monument to Grants, watch for the little road on your right to Bandera Crater and Ice Cave, near where the highway crosses the crest of the mountains. Several miles farther along, a big brown National Park Service sign marks the trailhead for the Zuñi-Ácoma Trail.

NM 53 brings you back to I-40 at the western Grants/ Milan exit. To see the other side of El Malpais, with the best views of the lava fields, take either the interstate or the business loop to the eastern Grants exit and follow NM 117 south for 10 miles to Sandstone Bluff Overlook and 7 more miles to La Ventana Natural Arch. Return to the interstate by the same route.

The exit to Ácoma is 15 miles east on I-40. Albuquerque is another 60 miles down the interstate.

Sightseeing Highlights

▲▲▲ **Petrified Forest National Park**—This colorful patch of apparent wasteland was a tropical forest 200 million years ago. Trees similar to California's giant redwoods grew along the shore of a sea that rose and receded over countless millennia to deposit multicolored layers of sediment, burying and petrifying parts of the forest. Wind and rain erosion have exposed the huge stone tree trunks and created the striking painted desert around them. The idea of primeval forest here, in a land where today scraggly clumps of grass struggle to survive, challenges the imagination. With the coming of the railroad in 1883, entrepreneurs began sawing and polishing petri-

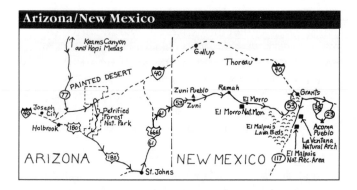

Arizona/New Mexico

fied wood to ship back east, where it was a fashionable
material for table tops. In just 16 years, they shipped out
over 20 million pounds of it. To stop the plunder, Theo-
dore Roosevelt declared the petrified forest a national
monument in 1899. It was raised to national park status in
1962. The National Park Service is very serious about
preventing the removal of petrified wood, and vehicles
are subject to search by rangers on the way out.

The most extensive petrified forest areas are in the
southern part of the park. Along the 27-mile scenic drive
from the south gate on US 180 to the north gate on I-40,
stop and walk through the strange landscape near the
Rainbow Forest Museum and at the Crystal Forest and Jas-
per Forest turnouts. Take the three-quarter-mile paved
walking trail among blue, white, and brown striped hills
from the fourth turnout on the one-way loop road at
Blue Mesa, midway through the park.

The park is open only during daylight hours. Admission is $5 per vehicle. There is no lodge or campground.
Food, gasoline, and souvenirs, including lots of petrified
wood imported from outside the park (keep your receipt
until you leave the park), are sold at the Painted Desert
Oasis by the visitors center at the north gate.

▲ **Zuñi Reservation**—The people who live here are
classified as Pueblo Indians, although their language is
not related to that of any other known Native American
tribe. They are best known for the costumed Shalako

house blessing ceremonies held around the beginning of December. Now mostly of modern construction, the town of Zuñi has been continuously occupied for 700 years. Ancient ruins around Zuñi were to become Zuñi-Cibola National Historic Park under a resolution passed by the U.S. Congress in 1988. Unfortunately, nobody consulted the Zuñi people about it until 1990, when they voted the plan down. The ruins remain closed to the non-Indian public. Although it has no national park, the reservation does have some pretty little fishing lakes.

▲▲ **El Morro National Monument**—America's first national monument (1906), El Morro was established to protect the many inscriptions scratched into the sandstone around a lovely oasis at the base of the 200-foot cliffs. Though wading and bathing are prohibited, the pool looks so inviting that it's no mystery why just about every southwestern expedition for three centuries stopped here. (Besides, it was the only water for miles around.) Observe how many Spanish conquistadors, whowrotewithoutspacesbetweenwords, recorded that their journeys were "a su cuesta" (at their own expense), and note the tombstonelike precision with which U.S. military explorers inscribed their graffiti. The earliest Spanish inscription (1605) is that of Don Juan de Oñate, who led the first settlers to New Mexico. Native American petroglyphs on the same rock are twice as old.

The best part of a visit to El Morro is the one-hour loop hike to the top of the rock, where you'll find the ruins of a small Anasazi pueblo with a magnificent view. Surprise: the cliff that looks so solid and massive from below is actually a wall, 200 feet high but just a few feet thick, separating the visitors center area from a box canyon.

The visitors center and trail are open daily from 8:00 a.m. to 7:00 p.m. in the summer months, until 5:00 p.m. the rest of the year. Admission is $1 per person, maximum $3 per vehicle. While at the visitors center, pick up information sheets on nearby, undeveloped El Malpais National Monument.

▲▲ **Bandera Crater and Ice Cave**—Hike about a mile to see Bandera Crater, one of five volcanoes that created

the El Malpais lava field. Nearby, another short trail leads
to an ice cave. The porous lava insulates an underground
pond, keeping it perpetually frozen; the cave is often 70
degrees cooler than the temperature on the surface. This
privately owned tourist attraction is presently being
acquired by the National Park Service as part of El Malpais
National Monument. It is the only developed facility
within the monument. Hours are 8:00 a.m. to 7:00 p.m.
during the summer months, until 4:00 p.m. the rest of the
year. Admission is $4 for adults, $2 for children ages 5 to 11.

▲ **El Malpais National Monument**—Created by act of
Congress in 1988, El Malpais is one of the nation's newest
national monuments. Because of tight National Park Service budgets in recent years, there have been no improve-
ments except for a few signs. The information center, in a
former gas station at 620 E. Santa Fe Street in Grants, can
furnish photocopied flyers on hiking and show you a
map of the area. Otherwise, you're on your own. Malpais,
Spanish for "badlands," is the name given to lava beds
throughout New Mexico. Three thousand years ago, a
row of volcanoes gushed a river of molten rock 30 miles
long and up to 20 miles wide.

You can hike along the edge of the lava beds, which are
quite different from those you saw at Sunset Crater, by
taking the Zuñi-Ácoma Trail, a fragment of the route that
once linked the two ancient pueblos. Although mostly
level, this trail is slow and difficult because of the rough
terrain. The trail itself is indistinct, so you must follow
marker posts. The marked portion of the trail runs for 7½
miles, but the first mile may be enough.

The best view of the lava field is from the opposite side
of the lava field at Sandstone Bluff Overlook on NM 117.
From there, continue to La Ventana to see the largest
accessible natural arch in New Mexico.

▲▲ **Ácoma (Sky City)**—Ácoma is the most impressively
situated of New Mexico's Indian pueblos as well as one of
the oldest and most traditional. Continuously inhabited
since A.D. 1075 (when Chaco Canyon was at its zenith),
Ácoma was one of the towns, along with Zuñi, that

inspired the "Seven Cities of Cibola" legend that drew
Coronado to explore the American Southwest in A.D.
1540 in search of rumored wealth surpassing that of the
Incas. (Was he disappointed!) The pueblo also has a Franciscan mission church dating from 1629 (older than San
Miguel, Santa Fe's "Oldest Church in the U.S."). Eighty
such missions were built in the 1600s, but only two sur-
vived the Pueblo Revolt of 1680. The other is at Isleta
Pueblo near Albuquerque.

While most Ácoma people now live in modern villages
below the mesa, the old pueblo remains the center of
religious life. Ácoma is on top of the 400-foot mesa, 13
miles by road from the interstate. No cars are permitted
beyond the tribal visitors center. Access is by shuttle bus.
The tours, which run hourly from 8:00 a.m. to 6:00 p.m.
during the summer months (shorter hours off-season)
cost $5 per adult, $4 for senior citizens, $3 for children
ages 7 to 17. Camera and sketching permit fees are the
highest of any Indian pueblo in New Mexico. The pueblo
is closed for religious ceremonies to which the public is
not invited on several days during the summer and fall.
For current schedule information, call ahead at (505)
252-1139.

Camping
El Morro has a small, pleasant campground among the
juniper trees. It only fills up on weekends. There is no
camping fee, though a donation box quietly solicits
voluntary contributions to help pay for the new rest
room.

In case you find the El Morro campground full, go to
the **Inscription Rock RV Park** about a mile farther
along New Mexico 53. Sites run $11 with full hookups,
$8 without.

Lodging
The closest motel accommodations are one hour's drive
beyond El Morro at the town of Grants on I-40. A faded
uranium mining center of the 1950s, Grants exists today

mainly as an overnight stop for trucks, and motel prices
are low enough to convince big-rig drivers to stay here
instead of rolling on into Albuquerque. Top of the line is
the **Best Western Inn**, (505) 287-7901, with in-room
movies, a whirlpool and sauna, and a café; doubles start
at about $64. In the moderate price range, the **Econo-
Lodge** (formerly the Holiday Inn), (505) 287-4426,
has doubles for $30, and the **Leisure Lodge** (formerly
the Travelodge), (505) 287-2991, has them for $33.
There are also about a dozen ma-and-pa motels where
you can get a decent room for about $20. If you're camp-
ing your way across the Southwest on a budget, you
won't find a cheaper shower, real bed, and cable color TV
anywhere. Look at the room first and make sure the
plumbing and TV work.

Food
There is a restaurant at Petrified Forest National Park but
none at El Morro. In fact, except for a small café in Zuñi,
there is no food to be found along this afternoon's route.
If you're camping, stock up on groceries in Holbrook or
St. Johns. Otherwise, the only restaurants around are in
Grants. After trying numerous family restaurants, fast-
food joints, and other dining possibilities around Grants,
the only place I can recommend wholeheartedly is the
Golden Skillet coffee shop in the truck stop 3 miles
west of town at the Milan exit from I-40. In case you want
to place a collect or credit card phone call home, there is
a telephone at each table. There are also pay showers,
video games, and a store that sells cowboy hats, boots,
huge belt buckles, auto repair tools, CB radios, portable
sound systems, C&W cassettes, paperback westerns, soft
drinks, beef jerky, silly postcards, the latest in radar detec-
tion technology—everything an interstate trucker needs.

Walk in Beauty
I'll leave you now, two hours drive down the interstate to
Albuquerque. I sincerely hope you've enjoyed your
southwestern trip as much as I've enjoyed sharing this
information with you. I welcome your comments, sug-

gestions, or discoveries. Write me c/o John Muir Publications, whose address appears in the last pages of this book.

Travel beckons us with pretty places and enchanting promises but leaves us, at the end, with experiences that can translate into a better understanding of our world. As you finish your southwestern trip, take a moment to think back on the meaning of what you've seen. Nobody has said it better than the Navajo singer of "Nahasdzaan Shima":

Earth My Mother,
We see you dressed in beautiful colors.
Father Sky provides beautiful things to you.
Like a man gives beautiful things to his wife.
Now we use up and destroy these beautiful things.
Now we are hurt because you are hurt.
You only ask us for blessings and respect;
You only expect us to work together in balance and
  harmony.
Earth My Mother,
We will return to you these gifts of beauty and grace.
We will return with beauty and grace.

INDEX

Other Books from John Muir Publications

Adventure Vacations: From Trekking in New Guinea to Swimming in Siberia, Bangs 256 pp. $17.95

Asia Through the Back Door, 3rd ed., Steves and Gottberg 326 pp. $15.95

Belize: A Natural Destination, Mahler, Wotkyns, Schafer 304 pp. $16.95

Bus Touring: Charter Vacations, U.S.A., Warren with Bloch 168 pp. $9.95

California Public Gardens: A Visitor's Guide, Sigg 304 pp. $16.95

Catholic America: Self-Renewal Centers and Retreats, Christian-Meyer 325 pp. $13.95

Costa Rica: A Natural Destination, 2nd ed., Sheck 288 pp. $16.95

Elderhostels: The Students' Choice, 2nd ed., Hyman 312 pp. $15.95

Environmental Vacations: Volunteer Projects to Save the Planet, 2nd ed., Ocko 248 pp. $16.95

Europe 101: History & Art for the Traveler, 4th ed., Steves and Openshaw 372 pp. $15.95

Europe Through the Back Door, 10th ed., Steves 448 pp. $16.95

A Foreign Visitor's Guide to America, Baldwin and Levine 200 pp. $10.95 (avail. 9/92)

Floating Vacations: River, Lake, and Ocean Adventures, White 256 pp. $17.95

Great Cities of Eastern Europe, Rapoport 256 pp. $16.95

Gypsying After 40: A Guide to Adventure and Self-Discovery, Harris 264 pp. $14.95

The Heart of Jerusalem, Nellhaus 336 pp. $12.95

Indian America: A Traveler's Companion, 2nd ed., Eagle/Walking Turtle 448 pp. $17.95

Interior Furnishings Southwest: The Sourcebook of the Best Production Craftspeople, Deats and Villani 256 pp. $19.95 (avail. 9/92)

Mona Winks: Self-Guided Tours of Europe's Top Museums, Steves and Openshaw 456 pp. $14.95

Opera! The Guide to Western Europe's Great Houses, Zietz 296 pp. $18.95

Paintbrushes and Pistols: How the Taos Artists Sold the West, Taggett and Schwarz 280 pp. $17.95

The People's Guide to Mexico, 8th ed., Franz 608 pp. $17.95

The People's Guide to RV Camping in Mexico, Franz with Rogers 320 pp. $13.95

Ranch Vacations: The Complete Guide to Guest and Resort, Fly-Fishing, and Cross-Country Skiing Ranches, 2nd ed., Kilgore 396 pp. $18.95

The Shopper's Guide to Art and Crafts in the Hawaiian Islands, Schuchter 272 pp. $13.95

The Shopper's Guide to Mexico, Rogers and Rosa 224 pp. $9.95

Ski Tech's Guide to Equipment, Skiwear, and Accessories, ed. Tanler 144 pp. $11.95

Ski Tech's Guide to Maintenance and Repair, ed. Tanler 160 pp. $11.95

A Traveler's Guide to Asian Culture, Chambers 224 pp. $13.95

Traveler's Guide to Healing Centers and Retreats in North America, Rudee and Blease 240 pp. $11.95

Understanding Europeans, Miller 272 pp. $14.95

Undiscovered Islands of the Caribbean, 2nd ed., Willes 232 pp. $14.95

Undiscovered Islands of the Mediterranean, 2nd ed., Moyer and Willes 256 pp. $13.95

Undiscovered Islands of the U.S. and Canadian West Coast, Moyer and Willes 208 pp. $12.95

A Viewer's Guide to Art: A Glossary of Gods, People, and Creatures, Shaw and Warren 144 pp. $10.95

2 to 22 Days Series

Each title offers 22 flexible daily itineraries that can be used to get the most out of vacations of any length. Included are not only "must see" attractions but also little-known villages and hidden "jewels" as well as valuable general information.

22 Days Around the World, 1992 ed., Rapoport and Willes 256 pp. $12.95 (**1993 ed.** avail. 8/92)

2 to 22 Days Around the Great Lakes, 1992 ed., Schuchter 192 pp. $9.95

22 Days in Alaska, Lanier 128 pp. $7.95

2 to 22 Days in the American Southwest, 1992 ed., Harris 176 pp. $9.95

2 to 22 Days in Asia, 1992 ed., Rapoport and Willes 176 pp. $9.95 (**1993 ed.** avail. 8/92)

2 to 22 Days in Australia, 1992 ed., Gottberg 192 pp. $9.95 (**1993 ed.** avail. 8/92)

2 to 22 Days in California, 1992 ed., Rapoport 192 pp. $9.95 (**1993 ed.** avail. 8/92)

22 Days in China, Duke and Victor 144 pp. $7.95

2 to 22 Days in Europe, 1992 ed., Steves 276 pp. $12.95

2 to 22 Days in Florida, 1992 ed., Harris 192 pp. $9.95 (**1993 ed.** avail. 8/92)

2 to 22 Days in France, 1992 ed., Steves 192 pp. $9.95

2 to 22 Days in Germany, Austria, & Switzerland, 1992 ed., Steves 224 pp. $9.95

2 to 22 Days in Great Britain, 1992 ed., Steves 192 pp. $9.95

2 to 22 Days in Hawaii, 1992 ed., Schuchter 176 pp. $9.95 (**1993 ed.** avail. 8/92)

22 Days in India, Mathur 136 pp. $7.95

22 Days in Japan, Old 136 pp. $7.95

22 Days in Mexico, 2nd ed., Rogers and Rosa 128 pp. $7.95

2 to 22 Days in New England, 1992 ed., Wright 192 pp. $9.95

2 to 22 Days in New Zealand, 1992 ed., Schuchter 176 pp. $9.95 (**1993 ed.** avail. 8/92)

2 to 22 Days in Norway, Sweden, & Denmark, 1992 ed., Steves 192 pp. $9.95

2 to 22 Days in the Pacific Northwest, 1992 ed., Harris 192 pp. $9.95

2 to 22 Days in the Rockies, 1992 ed., Rapoport 176 pp. $9.95

2 to 22 Days in Spain & Portugal, 1992 ed., Steves 192 pp. $9.95

2 to 22 Days in Texas, 1992 ed., Harris 192 pp. $9.95 (**1993 ed.** avail. 8/92)

2 to 22 Days in Thailand, 1992 ed., Richardson 176 pp. $9.95
(1993 ed. avail. 8/92)
22 Days in the West Indies, Morreale and Morreale 136 pp. $7.95

Parenting Series
Being a Father: Family, Work, and Self, *Mothering* Magazine
176 pp. $12.95
**Preconception: A Woman's Guide to Preparing for Pregnancy
and Parenthood,** Aikey-Keller 232 pp. $14.95
Schooling at Home: Parents, Kids, and Learning, *Mothering*
Magazine 264 pp. $14.95
Teens: A Fresh Look, *Mothering* Magazine 240 pp. $14.95

"Kidding Around" Travel Guides for Young Readers
Written for kids eight years of age and older.
Kidding Around Atlanta, Pedersen 64 pp. $9.95
Kidding Around Boston, Byers 64 pp. $9.95
Kidding Around Chicago, Davis 64 pp. $9.95
Kidding Around the Hawaiian Islands, Lovett 64 pp. $9.95
Kidding Around London, Lovett 64 pp. $9.95
Kidding Around Los Angeles, Cash 64 pp. $9.95
Kidding Around the National Parks of the Southwest, Lovett
108 pp. $12.95
Kidding Around New York City, Lovett 64 pp. $9.95
Kidding Around Paris, Clay 64 pp. $9.95
Kidding Around Philadelphia, Clay 64 pp. $9.95
Kidding Around San Diego, Luhrs 64 pp. $9.95
Kidding Around San Francisco, Zibart 64 pp. $9.95
Kidding Around Santa Fe, York 64 pp. $9.95
Kidding Around Seattle, Steves 64 pp. $9.95
Kidding Around Spain, Biggs 108 pp. $12.95
Kidding Around Washington, D.C., Pedersen 64 pp. $9.95

"Extremely Weird" Series for Young Readers
Written for kids eight years of age and older.
Extremely Weird Bats, Lovett 48 pp. $9.95
Extremely Weird Birds, Lovett 48 pp. $9.95
Extremely Weird Endangered Species, Lovett 48 pp. $9.95
Extremely Weird Fishes, Lovett 48 pp. $9.95
Extremely Weird Frogs, Lovett 48 pp. $9.95
Extremely Weird Primates, Lovett 48 pp. $9.95
Extremely Weird Reptiles, Lovett 48 pp. $9.95
Extremely Weird Spiders, Lovett 48 pp. $9.95

Masters of Motion Series
For kids eight years and older.
How to Drive an Indy Race Car, Rubel 48 pages $9.95 paper
(avail. 8/92)
How to Fly a 747, Paulson 48 pages $9.95 (avail. 9/92)
How to Fly the Space Shuttle, Shorto 48 pages $9.95 paper
(avail. 10/92)

Quill Hedgehog Adventures Series
Green fiction for kids. Written for kids eight years of age and older.
Quill's Adventures in the Great Beyond. Waddington-Feather
96 pp. $5.95
Quill's Adventures in Wasteland, Waddington-Feather 132 pp. $5.95
Quill's Adventures in Grozzieland, Waddington-Feather 132 pp. $5.95

X-ray Vision Series

For kids eight years and older.

Looking Inside Cartoon Animation, Schultz 48 pages $9.95 paper (avail. 9/92)
Looking Inside Sports Aerodynamics, Schultz 48 pages $9.95 paper (avail. 9/92)
Looking Inside the Brain, Schultz 48 pages $9.95 paper

Other Young Readers Titles

The Indian Way: Learning to Communicate with Mother Earth, McLain 114 pp. $9.95
The Kids' Environment Book: What's Awry and Why, Pedersen 192 pp. $13.95
Kids Explore America's Hispanic Heritage, Westridge Young Writers Workshop 112 pp. $7.95
Rads, Ergs, and Cheeseburgers: The Kids' Guide to Energy and the Environment, Yanda 108 pp. $12.95

Automotive Titles

How to Keep Your VW Alive, 14th ed., 440 pp. $21.95
How to Keep Your Subaru Alive 480 pp. $21.95
How to Keep Your Toyota Pickup Alive 392 pp. $21.95
How to Keep Your Datsun/Nissan Alive 544 pp. $21.95
The Greaseless Guide to Car Care Confidence: Take the Terror Out of Talking to Your Mechanic, Jackson 224 pp. $14.95
Off-Road Emergency Repair & Survival, Ristow 160 pp. $9.95

Ordering Information

If you cannot find our books in your local bookstore, you can order directly from us. Please check the "Available" date above. If you send us money for a book not yet available, we will hold your money until we can ship you the book. Your books will be sent to you via UPS (for U.S. destinations). UPS will not deliver to a P.O. Box; please give us a street address. Include $3.75 for the first item ordered and $.50 for each additional item to cover shipping and handling costs. For airmail within the U.S., enclose $4.00. All foreign orders will be shipped surface rate; please enclose $3.00 for the first item and $1.00 for each additional item. Please inquire about foreign airmail rates.

Method of Payment

Your order may be paid by check, money order, or credit card. We cannot be responsible for cash sent through the mail. All payments must be made in U.S. dollars drawn on a U.S. bank. Canadian postal money orders in U.S. dollars are acceptable. For VISA, MasterCard, or American Express orders, include your card number, expiration date, and your signature, or call (800) 888-7504. Books ordered on American Express cards can be shipped only to the billing address of the cardholder. Sorry, no C.O.D.'s. Residents of sunny New Mexico, add 5.875% tax to the total.

Address all orders and inquiries to:
John Muir Publications
P.O. Box 613
Santa Fe, NM 87504
(505) 982-4078
(800) 888-7504